T·H·E

EXPERT'S GUIDE

TO BACKYARD

BIRDFEEDING

Bill Adler, Jr.,
and Heidi Hughes

CROWN PUBLISHERS, INC.,

NEW YORK

To my sister, Diane, who grew up with me in New York City and still can't believe that I've written a book about birds

BILL ADLER, JR.

To Tommy Valega, the bird watcher from Tremley Point, New Jersey

HEIDI HUGHES

Photography Credits

BILL ADLER, JR.: Pp. 16 right, 28 right, 29, 36 all, 39, 41 right, 52, 64 all, 100, 139, and 165 top; ASPECTS: 25 upper and lower right, and 65 bottom; JAMES BEARDS PHOTOGRAPHY: 160 all; BOWER COMPANY: 14; ARTHUR BROWN COMPANY: 20 upper left; RICHARD CLARK: 161–162 all; KARL COOK: 16 left, 18–19, 20 right and lower left, 28 left, 33, 34 all, 38, 41 upper and lower left, 45 all, 48 all, 72–73 all, 75 all, 77–78, 80, 99, 103–105 all, 107 all, 116 all, 118 all, 120, 134 right, 136 upper left and upper right, 138 all, 140 bottom, 141 right, 144 all, 146 all, 148 all, and 157 all; DROLL YANKEE: 60 top; DUNCRAFT: 60 bottom; FADCO: 31 left; KAMCAST: 114; KARLSBURG COMPANY: 54; OPUS: 43 left; SAMSON: 132; J. L. WADE NATURE HOUSE: 153 all; and WILDWOOD FARMS: 168 upper right, and 170 left.

Published by Crown Publishers, Inc., 201 East 50th Street, New York, New York 10022. Member of the Crown Publishing Group.

CROWN is a trademark of Crown Publishers, Inc.

Manufactured in the United States of America

Library of Congress Cataloging-in-Publication Data

Adler, Bill, 1956–
    The expert's guide to backyard birdfeeding : the indispensable guide to everything for the birds / by Bill Adler Jr. and Heidi Hughes.
        p.   cm.
        1. Birds, Attracting of—Miscellanea.   I. Hughes, Heidi.
    II. Title.
QL676.5.A33   1990
598'.07'234—dc20   89-24003
                                                                                            CIP

ISBN 0-517-57495-0

10 9 8 7 6 5 4 3 2

CONTENTS

ACKNOWLEDGMENTS

A book like *The Expert's Guide to Backyard Birdfeeding* is the product of not just the authors but many minds. Our first thanks go to Peggy Robin and Tommy Valega, who, forgoing summers of backyard barbecuing, let their homes and yards become bird-product testing centers. Our agent, Jane Dystel, was as always of immeasurable help and encouragement during this entire project. Crown Publishing's ace editor Lisa Healy was always ready and able to give helpful and insightful advice. Without the advice of Joanne Klappauf and Arthur Brown we might not have been able to get started at all. Many of the photographs in this book were taken by Karl Cook, who donated his time and talent. We also thank the thousands of Wild Bird Company customers for asking all those questions about bird gadgets. Thanks, too, to Bruce Taylor of the Wetsel Seed Company for providing contacts at bird companies. Bob Horsnell gave a critical eye to this manuscript and helped mind the store while we were at work. Dave McCutcheon and Dave Pelascek of Bay-Mor Pet Feeds taught us much about the bird-seed industry. Julie Dunwoody worked hard on this project as well. Without Janet Ford's comments this book would read a lot rougher. Warren Lewis helped us focus on the important issue of birding, and Renee DuBois watched out for the numbers. Nobel Wakabayashi helped with the bird seed. Thanks also to Steve Cox and Mauricio Suarez for their carpentry skills, and to Dorothy and Jon Hughes for doing everything they could to make things easier for us.

INTRODUCTION

The essence of birdfeeding is birds. That's what our hobby—actually passion—is all about. We're dazzled by the colors, shapes, and faces of birds, delighted by their willingness to eat from the tables we set for them, enchanted by their songs, and entertained by their curious behavior.

It's an easy hobby, too. Just toss out some seed and *voilà*—there are wild birds in your backyard. A bird identification book, perhaps a pair of binoculars, and you have everything you need to appreciate birds. The only other element that occasionally seems necessary to enjoy birdfeeding is an enthusiastic (or at least willing) spouse, who will come to the window when you cry, "There's a pileated woodpecker at the suet feeder!"

Pity all those stamp collectors, needlepointers, model race-car builders, rock climbers, ham radio operators, Barbie-doll collectors, and scuba divers whose hobbies cost hundreds or thousands of dollars in specialized equipment or require them to travel thousands of miles. Even bird*watchers*—those hardy folks who like to visit distant forests and mountains lugging fifty-pound lenses, wide-angle binoculars, thermoses of coffee, field guides, and a not-so-enthusiastic spouse—have to expend money, energy, and time pursuing their pastime.

What could be an easier, more relaxing, more fulfilling hobby than feeding wild birds? What other hobby could simultaneously give animals an edge in an environment altered by humans, be educational, and also be fun?

But after a time even an exuberant spouse isn't enough to sustain the hobby. Eventually, merely watching birds pick up food scattered throughout the yard doesn't seem like a hobby anymore.

People who feed birds want more. They want birding paraphernalia just as the stamp collectors have their magnifying glasses and the scuba divers have their gauges and rubber suits. A hobby has to have its equipment to make it a full-fledged pastime.

Thus enter center stage: birdfeeders, birdbaths, specialized birdseeds, birdhouses, birdbath warmers, antisquirrel devices, squirrel feeders, seed storage silos, scoops for thistle seed, scoops for sunflower seed, one-way mirrored feeders, a dozen different poles for feeders, birdhouses that cost more than human houses, feeders made out of soda bottles, feeders made out of material that seems similar to the exterior of the space shuttle . . .

Now that's a hobby!

Move over stamp collectors. You have nothing that can compare to the stuff that birders can buy.

Even if it were only for the fun of it, all these bird gadgets would be great. More and more sophisticated feeders to outwit squirrels, birdhouses that attract bluebirds and keep predators away, seed that only goldfinches like, seed that only blue jays like, birdbaths that look like museum-quality sculptures, birdbaths that have built-in heaters for winter, feeders that can feed twenty birds at a time, feeders that feed a single bird at a time—all of these products are made more or less with one purpose in mind: to entertain humans.

But bird gadgets have a more important purpose than providing the backbone of the second most popular hobby in the country. Over the centuries we have taken away a considerable portion of the habitat of various animals including birds. We've destroyed their shelters; ruined potential nesting sites; taken away many of the streams and lakes they drink from; poisoned their environment with pesticides, oil spills, and a myriad of unimaginable chemicals; decimated sources of food; and disrupted their overall environment.

Feeding birds, offering water, and providing shelter are the least we can do.

Yet not all bird gadgets are good for birds. (Not all are good for humans, either. We'll get to that in a moment.) Many feeders aren't protected against rain, so they allow seed to get wet which, in turn, causes seed to become dangerously moldy. Other feeders are designed in such a way as to allow bird droppings to accumulate on the seed, which can become a medium for bacterial growth. Feeders, as they empty, can lure birds inside. The same sort of thing is true for other bird products. Some birdhouses get super-hot in the sunshine and some aren't secure against predators. Not all birdseed is equally effective in attracting birds.

Likewise, there's a wide disparity in the quality of birdfeeding products as they affect humans. Some are brilliantly designed. Others are, well, silly and stupid. A few birdfeeders have to be filled every day (if you're lucky); others are constructed in such a way that their contents barely last a day (or through the first squirrel attack, whichever comes first). Many birdfeeders are open invitations to squirrels, while others are virtually impregnable to these hungry, persistent critters. Birdfeeders can be either easy to fill or such a pain that you end up deciding to let the birds fend for themselves.

Many birdhouses are easy to clean; but a good number aren't, and these must be thrown away, something that doesn't sit well with a recycling conscience. Poles, baffles, suction-cup window feeders, seed scoops—each product has its advantages and disadvantages. Who wants to buy a pole only to find that there aren't many feeders that will fit on top?

What we figured when we came up with the idea for *The Expert's Guide to Backyard Birdfeeding* was that it's much better to know all this information *before* you buy a bird gadget: better for the birds and better for the humans.

The Expert's Guide isn't comprehensive—nothing could be, because there are new bird devices invented all the time—but it's the closest thing to a complete guide for the feeder of wild birds that there is.

BIRDFEEDERS

When the ground is covered with snow and ice, it's easiest to toss seed out the door: the lazy person's birdfeeder. But it's healthier for the birds to get their "handouts" at a formal feeding station, off the ground. One of the benefits of feeding wild birds is that when your friends with dogs are out walking their pets in freezing rain and snow, all you have to do is go out and fill the feeder, then sit back and watch your birds from the comfort of your warm kitchen.

But it is mostly for the health of birds that you should use a feeder. Regardless of the season, food that sits on the ground for even a short time is exposed to potential contamination by dampness, mold, bacteria, animal droppings, and lawn chemicals.

There's no law that says birdfeeders have to be fancy. You can start simply with a piece of scrap wood, elevated a few inches above the ground on a pole. Add a few holes for drainage and *voilà*—you've built a platform feeder. It won't be long before the birds find it.

Whether you build a feeder or not, eventually you'll find yourself looking at commercially manufactured feeders. There's a gigantic variety to choose from. And these feeders fulfill a variety of functions. Some let only small birds eat; some hold peanuts, but not thistle; other feeders have such a large capacity that you may only have to fill them every few weeks; and still others require that you tend

them daily. A few feeders are designed with
while others are more suited to a moonscape.
ity and bird safety, too. There are hundreds
do you make the "right" choice? What is it
"good?"

This chapter is about seed feeders; suet h
fruit feeders are discussed later.

Placement

First consider placement. Different feeders are designed for different placements. Where do you want to watch your birds? From a
kitchen window? A sliding glass door opening onto a deck? A
second-story window? If you put a feeder in the yard but your bedroom window overlooks the other side of the house, you may be
doing the birds a big favor but you won't be deriving that much pleasure from feeding birds. If there's a trade-off between having the
world's fanciest feeder and getting a close-up view of birds, choose
the view.

Pick a location that has year-round easy access *for you*. In harsh
weather, when the birds are most vulnerable, you may be reluctant
to climb a ladder to fill a feeder hanging from a branch that's at
second-story level.

Also consider the *mess* factor. Birds may be pretty, but what they
leave behind at the feeder is not. Pick a location where discarded
seed hulls and bird droppings won't be a clean-up problem. Also,
you may not want to place a feeder full of black-oil sunflower on
your lawn because sunflower hulls leach an acid that kills grass.

Put your feeders where the squirrels can't reach them. (See section on squirrel-proof feeders later in this chapter.) Those cute
rodents like sunflower and peanuts as much or more than acorns.
Squirrels will take over birdfeeders, scaring the birds away, scat-
tering seed around, and sometimes eating a feeder for dessert.
(Squirrels like wooden feeders best, but are more than happy to
sharpen their teeth on plastic and metal feeders. If you don't believe

quirrels will change your mind.) All it takes is one uppity
. If you've seen squirrels in your neighborhood, it's a sure
at they will visit your feeder.

quirrels are incredibly agile and strong. They can leap up four
eet or more, swim, and chew through most anything you put in
their path. Any feeder hanging from a tree, with or without a squirrel guard or baffle, is likely to become a squirrel feeder.

There are ways to thwart squirrels. Putting your feeder on a pole
protected by a baffle is one of the least aggravating solutions. There
are several varieties of squirrel-proof poles that can aid in protecting
your feeder, which are described later. The most effective squirrel-
proof feeders are the pole-mounted metal "house" type. Strategi-
cally placed window feeders are also often effective against squirrels, because the only thing squirrels can't climb is glass.

Think long and hard before you hang anything from a tree limb.
Squirrels can jump amazing distances downward and laterally. If
you must hang a feeder, select a tube protected with metal mesh.
Most plastic "squirrel-proof" feeders, regardless of manufacturers'
claims, eventually succumb to rodent teeth. You may thwart the
squirrels for a little while with baffles hung from trees or strung
on a line between trees. (You can never have too many baffles.) But
eventually the furry little rodents figure a way to get to your seed.*

Once you've determined where you're going to put your feeder,
you're ready to go shopping. Besides a feeder's squirrel-proof capa-
bility, several other criteria are important including:

- How does the feeder look in your yard?
- How durable is it?
- Will it keep the seeds dry?
- How easy is it to clean?

*The best source of information about preventing squirrel attacks is *Outwitting Squirrels:
101 Cunning Stratagems to Reduce Dramatically the Egregious Misappropriation of Seed
from Your Birdfeeder by Squirrels*, by Bill Adler, Jr., Chicago Review Press, $8.95.

- How much seed will it hold?
- How many birds will it feed at one time?
- Which species will use the feeder?

Esthetics

How a feeder looks is purely a matter of taste. Most people who feed wild birds (and some manufacturers, it seems) don't care too much about the way the feeder looks; what they are interested in is the way the *birds* look. Yet there is a wide selection of colors, shapes, and sizes among feeders. How you position a feeder also makes a difference in what it looks like. You may have to trade off some other feature such as durability or size to get the feeder that's most attractive for your yard. We don't have much else to say about esthetics, because that's up to you. But keep this in mind: whatever feeder you select you will be looking at all the time.

Durability

There seems to be no end to the materials used in making bird-feeders. You can buy disposable plastic-bag feeders; feeders made of cloth, nylon, vinyl, and metal netting; acrylic, Plexiglas, Lexan, and PVC plastic tubes; ceramic and terra-cotta; redwood, western cedar, birch, pine, and plywood; aluminum, sheet metal, and aluminized steel; glass tubes and bottles. Just about the only material that's *not* used to construct birdfeeders is Kevlar, the stuff that bullet-proof vests are made of.

How long a feeder lasts depends on how much effort you put into maintaining it, the effects of the weather, whether squirrels can get to it, and how securely it's hung or mounted.

Of the plastics, polycarbonate (General Electric's trademarked formula is Lexan) is the most durable. When it comes to wood, we recommend western cedar over redwood because it resists insects, weathers well, and will survive rigorous cleaning. (It also takes centuries to replenish majestic redwood trees.) In the metal category, rust-resistant aluminized steel is a best buy.

Keeping Seeds Dry

Water can get into any feeder regardless of how carefully you protect it. Seed will rapidly spoil when it gets damp or wet, producing harmful molds or toxins. While cloth, vinyl, nylon, and metal netting feeders are inexpensive, they do not protect your seed. You can improve the weather resistance of a feeder by adding a plastic dome.

Most wood, plastic, ceramic, and metal feeders will keep seed dry, but water can seep into the feeding portals. Look for feeders with drainage holes in the bottoms of both the hopper and the tray.

Bowl-type feeders and feeder trays with tiny drainage holes may look great, but they will clog with seed and bird droppings, as well as accumulate moisture from rainwater—an unhealthy broth. Look for shallow platelike seed catchers that are attached to the feeder. The purpose of a tray is to catch dropped seeds while allowing spent seed hulls to blow away.

Cleaning

As any zookeeper or caged-bird owner will tell you, when you feed birds in a confined area, you have to expect bird droppings, feathers, an occasional insect or two, and leftover food mess. While you don't have to wash your feeders daily, you should clean them regularly.

Bacteria like salmonella can grow in your feeder, tray, and on the ground below, where moldy, wet seed and bird droppings accumulate. Birds can also pick up diseases transmitted by sick birds visiting your feeding station.

It's a good idea to move your feeders (just a foot or so) each season to give the ground underneath time to assimilate the seed debris and droppings.

Keeping your feeders clean should not be a major undertaking. The degree of maintenance required is directly related to the types of feeders and the birds you want to attract.

A thistle feeder for goldfinches should be cleaned about once a month, depending on how often it rains. Hummingbird feeders require cleaning at least every week, preferably two or three times a week. Sunflower and suet feeders may need to be cleaned only once a season.

Feeders made of plastic, ceramic, and glass are easy to clean. Wash them in a bucket of hot, soapy water fortified with chlorine bleach, or give them a run through your dishwasher.

Use the same regimen with wood and metal feeders, but substitute another disinfectant for the bleach so the wood won't fade.

Food Capacity

The ideal feeder capacity varies with your situation and the types of birds you want to attract.

If you feed hummingbirds, big feeders are not always better. One hummingbird will drink more than twice its body weight—about three grams a day. Early in the season, hummers are territorial and won't share a feeder. A sixteen-ounce feeder can be wasteful, or indeed lethal, because artificial nectar—sugar water—will ferment in the hot summer sun. Hummingbirds don't get drunk when they drink that much alcohol. They die.

If you see only one hummer in your yard, a two-ounce feeder is more than enough. On the other hand, if you live in the Southwest and have thirty-four hummers in your yard, a sixteen-ounce feeder may not be big enough. (Hummingbird feeders are discussed in more detail in a later chapter.)

If you opt for a large-volume seed feeder, be sure to protect it from the weather and keep it clean. If, after months of use, the birds suddenly abandon your feeder full of seed, it's time for a cleaning.

Wrong Birds at Your Feeder?

If crowding at your feeder becomes a problem, you can control the number of birds by putting out smaller amounts of seed, by using specialty seeds, or by using restrictive feeders that cater only to the specific birds you want to see.

If you don't fill your feeder when it's empty, the birds will look for food elsewhere. Not to worry. Even if it's a day or two between fillings, your birds will eventually return.

You can virtually eliminate visits by birds you'd rather not see by offering only certain seeds.

Let's suppose you're using black oil sunflower seed in a house-shaped feeder. It's November and your feeder has been taken over by house finches. You'd rather feed only cardinals, doves, and white-throated sparrows. Switch from black oil sunflower seed to safflower seed.

If you want only goldfinches, house finches, pine siskins, and an occasional dove and white-throated sparrow, try niger thistle in a thistle tube with a tray.

If you want only titmice and small woodpeckers, try peanut kernels in a starling-resistant peanut feeder.

If it's blue jays you want, fill a feeder with whole peanuts.

Several feeders are designed to restrict access to selected birds. These feeders have vertical perches or no perches at all, small feeding portals, or access only at the bottom so the birds have to eat upside down.

The most nonselective feeders are the tray, platform, or house-shaped feeders. You can encourage more small birds with feeders designed to keep out large birds. Wood tray feeders with vertical dowels and plastic feeders covered with wire mesh frustrate jays and doves.

You can modify your tube feeders to do the same thing. Just take off the seed trays. Remove the perches, and you've further selected only those birds capable of clinging: finches, chickadees, titmice, and woodpeckers.

Add vertical perches to tube thistle feeders, and you'll limit accessibility primarily to goldfinches.

If starlings are a problem at your suet feeder, you can discourage them by using a suet feeder with access only at the bottom. Starlings are reluctant to perch upside down. Chickadees, nuthatches, and woodpeckers have no problem feeding upside down.

The species you attract is determined primarily by the seeds you offer. The most effective way to attract the largest variety of birds to your yard is to put out separate feeders for each food:

- tube (with a tray) or house feeder for sunflower seed
- tube feeder for thistle seed
- house or platform feeder for millet
- starling-resistant suet feeder for woodpeckers
- bluebird feeder
- stationary or tray fruit feeder
- large or small perch nectar feeder
- wire-mesh cage feeder for peanuts
- window feeder with hulled sunflower

Rating the Products

Wooden Feeders

Say the word "birdfeeder" and most people think of a wooden houselike structure hanging from a tree near their kitchen window.

Everyone loves wooden feeders. And why not? They look a whole lot better than plastic and metal feeders. They don't get cloudy as plastic feeders do, don't get the paint chipped off as metal feeders do. They're more natural looking. Let's face it: Lexan does not go with tulips and spinach patches; wood does.

We concede that wooden feeders are attractive, but unfortunately they are susceptible to the same problems as wooden kitchen cutting boards. Both are very likely to harbor food-borne bacteria. What's worse, wooden birdfeeders can also harbor diseases transmitted by bird droppings.

Still, wooden birdfeeders look a whole lot better than easy-to-clean plastic and metal products. What can you do if you want a wooden feeder, and you're concerned about sanitation? Pick a feeder that has adequate drainage (so water does not wick up the feeder hopper), a narrow feed dispensing area (so birds can't get into the seed hopper and defecate on the seed), and a large dowel perch an inch or so away from the seed dispenser. (You might also consider *not* baffling your feeder so that squirrels can munch away at it; this way you'll have to replace it before the feeder can become contaminated.)

If you're going to buy or build a wooden feeder, be sure to look at what it's made of: wood, adhesives, staples, screws, or nails. Western red cedar is a best buy. It's economical and weather resistant. We don't recommend stained and chemically treated wood because the chemicals may leach into the feed. Put your nose close to a hot feeder and you can smell the petro-chemicals. Pine painted with exterior latex house paint is an inexpensive, safe alternative.

Quality feeders are fastened with wood adhesives and reinforced with galvanized steel or brass screws. Nails and staples are less expensive, but don't expect them to last as long as screw-reinforced feeders.

The most difficult problem with house-style feeders is keeping them from the squirrels. Most manufacturers want you to hang them from a tree (they come with built-in chain or rope hangers). Others wisely recommend mounting the feeders on poles. Unless you're prepared to accept squirrels, mount them on a pole.

There are literally hundreds of wooden feeders on the market. They come in all sorts of designs, with all sorts of promises. Your best buy is unstained, ¾-inch western red cedar, with plastic hoppers.

Look for a feeder with a hinged top that swings up for easy filling. We don't recommend feeders that fill through little holes in the roof. No matter what the manufacturer uses to plug up the roof, it will leak and eventually you'll lose the plug.

See that the plastic hopper plates are only about ½ inch from the floor. If they are any higher, chickadees are likely to push their way inside to get to that last seed. Unless there's a large gap between the roof and top of the plastic hopper, the bird cannot escape and is likely to flail itself to death trying.

A wooden or plastic inverted-V-shaped wedge in the center of the hopper floor will help direct the seed flow out, so as not to tempt a break-in. Plastic floors and perches go a long way to making wooden houses more sanitary and durable.

Bower Grand Estate Feeder

The Grand Estate Feeder, by Bower Company, is an "investment." It's that expensive. The feeder with post and baffle retails for over $200. This ostentatious feeder holds over ten pounds of seed and sports two side gaskets for suet. The frame is made of cast aluminum with a cast-iron look. A redwood roof shelters the large (23-inch) feeding area.

If there's a problem with this feeder, it's size. It's just too big. It can be a hassle to fill, and it may hold too much seed for its own good. Some of the seed that goes unreached by birds in their feeding and by you in your cleaning is likely to sprout or rot. In addition, bird droppings can accumulate on the perching platform.

Mill Store O-B3B

We can't say that we really like the name, but Mill Store Products' O-B3B is a basic, workable feeder. Nothing fancy, nothing special. The O-B3B is designed to feed birds and that's what it does.

Because the O-B3B is constructed of pine and plastic, expect it to last only a couple of seasons. If the squirrels don't do it in, the elements will. But it's not an expensive feeder, so you shouldn't feel

The Bower Grand Estate Feeder

too bad about disposing of it. Wooden feeders ought to be disposed of occasionally; wood on feeders is a breeding ground for diseases.

For some reason, birds seem to like this wooden hanging feeder. Among the five feeders that we were testing along with the O-B3B, birds ignored all the others and dined only at the O-B3B. Perhaps it's because it looks *natural*; or maybe the clear plastic sides let birds see the seed from a distance. Also, birds are more accustomed to hanging out in trees than among plastic tubes and metal boxes.

The O-B3B doesn't hold much seed—only a couple of cups. You should keep it filled at all times, too. The opening between the plastic hopper and platform is large enough for gluttonous chickadees to get inside and become trapped.

By the way, the O-B3B's pine is unfinished, so you can paint it any color you want.

Mill Store O-B7B

The O-B7B is the big cousin of the O-B3B. The two are almost identical, save for the size and for four dowel posts that protrude up from the corners of the O-B7B. They're supposed to be for holding suet.

Bruce Barber Feeders

If you simply have to have a wooden feeder, and you want one that looks terrific but lacks the excesses of the Grand Estate Feeder, then get a Bruce Barber feeder. Made from kiln-dried, sanded western red cedar, these "house" feeders are handcrafted by cabinetmakers in northwestern Pennsylvania. Barber feeders are made in sizes to hold from two cups to two gallons. Held together with brass thumb screws, these feeders should last a decade or two.

The Barber platform feeder not only is attractive but is one of the few platform feeders designed to keep seed dry.

All Barber feeders have adequate drainage and perching dowels large enough to make any cardinal comfortable, yet far enough away from the hopper to keep them from dirtying the hopper.

Mill Store Combo Suet/Seed Birdfeeder

You have to admit that this is an ingenious and handsome feeder. The Combo Suet/Seed Birdfeeder, by Mill Store Products, holds one pound of seed (sunflower, safflower, or shelled peanuts) *and* suet. So you can entertain both seed and suet eaters such as woodpeckers, nuthatches, Carolina wrens, and squirrels.

If you're interested in keeping the latter at bay, you will have to baffle this feeder very well because it contains no built-in squirrel defenses. This birdfeeder is like leaving a candy store open and unattended next to an elementary school. It is best mounted on a pole, but be sure the pole is away from trees. Once squirrels get

A feeder by Bruce Barber

The Mill Store Products Combo Suet/Seed Birdfeeder

to it, they not only will have unlimited access to the seed but will gnaw at the soft pine.

The Combo Suet/Seed Birdfeeder is an easy feeder to fill; just lift the hinged top and pour the seed in. Filling the suet nook is a little more difficult, however; commercial suet cakes are too big to fit into the compartment; they must be cut first. (If you store your suet cakes in the freezer, this is not a fun task.)

The Combo Suet/Seed Birdfeeder is designed to give birds easy access to seed. Unfortunately, birds can also defecate in the seed compartment, so it's important to clean the feeder regularly.

The Combo Suet/Seed Birdfeeder comes either stained or unstained, so you can paint the feeder any color. Birds can eat out of only one side of the feeder, so they will always be in view.

Cedarline Feeders

Cedarline wood feeders are made of ¾-inch white Michigan cedar stained with a gray preservative. After a summer in the sun, they'll look white. Most are held together with staples, some with screws; none are glued. Their moderately priced product line boggles the mind: double-decker, ten-pounder, two compartments, seed and suet, one-sider, five-pounder, twenty-pounder, platform, platform with a roof, donut holder, squirrel pole, squirrel platform, oriole orange feeder, bluebird feeder, one-fill (holds thirty pounds), starling-resistant suet feeder, suet log, woodpecker tail prop suet feeder, and peanut butter and jelly feeder.

Woodline Feeders

The three Woodline feeders are cute, stained brown feeders with red or green stained roofs. The two basic feeders hold five pounds, or two and a half pounds of seed each. The combo model holds a cup or two of seed, half a cake of suet on one side, and half an orange on the other. These inexpensive feeders are fastened with staples, so don't expect them to last forever.

Aspects Feeders

The Aspects Company also manufacturers white cedar feeders, stained silver-gray. The platform feeder measures 16 by 20 inches and comes with a short black metal pole. The small cedar feeder is 12 inches long and holds four quarts of seed. While the large cedar feeder (20 inches long) has two separate chambers, don't be tempted to use two different seeds.

Marsh Creek Feeders

Charlie Rouse at Marsh Creek makes a handsome hanging western cedar/wire-mesh tube for sunflower. This inexpensive feeder holds about four cups of seed and quickly attracts chickadees, titmice, nuthatches, finches, and woodpeckers.

Hyde Feeders

The Hyde Company manufactures several wood feeders. Their most popular are the Filling Station Combination and Sundeck Feeders. The Filling Station is made of 1-inch pine with dowels at either end for suet or fruit. It's a tight squeeze, since the dowels are a tad too close for most commercial suet cakes.

The nice things about this package are the low price and that it comes boxed complete with a 6-foot pole and polycarbonate squirrel

The Bird-in-Hand Feeder

baffle. On the down side, the Filling Station has a tiny filling hole on the roof that's bound to break in a couple of months. The roof does not cover the seed reservoir, so when it rains water is likely to wick up the hopper and spoil the seed. Add some large drainage holes to compensate for this. The pole will rust in about a year.

The Sun Deck feeder is a pretty redwood house-style feeder with a wide perching area on one side only. It invites birds to jump right into the seed. Be sure to add some large holes in the corners of the platform to facilitate drainage. The centerboard on the roof removes for filling.

Bird-in-Hand Feeder

Charlie Rouse, the inventor of this feeder, obviously has a wonderful sense of humor. Besides dispensing a variety of seeds, (black oil sunflower works best) the Bird-in-Hand actually trains chickadees and titmice to eat out of your hand.

Little Lake Industries Four Seasons Feeder

If squirrels get to this feeder, there probably won't be much of it left after a couple of weeks. Because the Four Seasons is designed to hold suet and seed, every squirrel in the neighborhood is going to try to reach it. Keep in mind that chickadees will try to squeeze between the plastic and wood to get at small amounts of seed that remain, so always keep this feeder filled.

The Little Lake Industries
Four Seasons Feeder

Tray Feeders

All seed-eating birds are likely to visit a tray feeder. No matter how high you put the tray, the birds that visit will depend on which seeds you offer. If you want to attract pheasants, quail, ducks, and geese, put fine cracked corn on a tray a couple of inches off the ground.

While a tray feeder has the advantage of attracting the largest variety of birds, it's the most difficult feeder to keep full and clean. (Don't rely on the rain to do the job for you.)

The Arthur C. Brown Company has the best solution we've seen so far: a house window screen in a red cedar frame. The screen mesh is small enough to keep even millet from falling through. All you do to clean it is pop it off the pole, scrub it with soap or bleach, then hose it down.

Tray feeders are the simplest in design and the easiest to fill. They're not terribly squirrel resistant and the seed becomes wet whenever it rains. Still, these feeders attract a large variety of birds who consume seed rapidly. Platform feeders are good buys when they have drainage holes.

Plastic Tube Feeders

There are hundreds of plastic tube feeders on the market. Design and choice of materials distinguish them and a careful eye can find subtle differences in the tubes themselves; the portals, perches, caps (tops), hangers; and the seed trays, poles, and squirrel baffles.

Tubes are made from a variety of materials including polycarbonate and several types of less "squirrel-proof" plastic including styrene, acrylic, and Plexiglas.

A typical tray feeder

A typical plastic tube feeder

A Bruce Barber feeder

Polycarbonate is the most durable. It will survive years of bird pecking. The other plastics are more likely to break up after only a few years of normal use. They're also easily chewed up by squirrels. If the squirrels and birds don't do them in, the cheaper plastics cloud and become brittle after several years' exposure to the elements.

Superior feeders have metal feeding portals. Better than any other material, metal withstands the daily rigors of bird pecking. Unfortunately, metal portals do not deter squirrels from devouring the plastic part of the tubes, but may encourage them to go to easier-to-attack feeders in your neighbor's yard.

When you buy a tube feeder, look for feeding portals small enough (less than 1 inch in diameter) to keep even the tiniest birds from getting their heads or bodies caught as they go after the few seeds that may sit below the bottom feeding portals. Also, look for portals with metal seed baffles inside the feeder to help minimize seed spillage.

Perches are made of wood, plastic, or metal. Metal is the most durable. Birds have a very efficient system of regulating body heat through their feet, so they won't freeze to the metal. (Without this ability to keep their feet from freezing, imagine how difficult life would be for penguins.)

Some feeder manufacturers put plastic sleeves on their metal perches. The birds don't need them, so why pay for the extra parts?

Tube feeders are gravity fed. Some have inverted V-shaped funnels above the bottom perches. These help keep seeds from piling up under the bottom feeding portals, where they spoil and are likely to drive birds crazy when they try to reach the seed.

Some feeders have patented seed distribution systems with shelves to keep seed evenly available at all the portals. The trick with these feeders is cleaning them without breaking them.

Manufacturers claim their so-called compartmentalized feeders, combo feeders, and triple-tube feeders attract many different birds. In theory, one feeder dispensing several different seeds is a great idea. In reality, it just doesn't work.

To understand why, you have to think like a bird. Birds prefer some seeds over others. If you've put out a triple-tube feeder with one tube for thistle, one for sunflower and one for mixed seed, you've probably noticed that the sunflower tube goes empty first, then the mix (with most of the seeds kicked to the ground), leaving the thistle tube to sit for weeks, where it more than likely rots.

If you have or want a triple tube, combo, or compartmentalized feeder, you're better off using only sunflower seed in it, because sunflower will attract the greatest variety of birds.

Droll Yankee A-6

The Droll Yankee Company makes what well may be the best-quality tube feeders on the market today. The A-6 (two-quart size) and larger capacity B-7 (four-quart size) are made of polycarbonate with metal feeding portals and perches.

The Droll Yankee feeders have the perfect cap. You'll never drop it when you fill the feeder on a cold winter day, because it's attached to the hanger. You can fill them easily with just about any funnel or seed dispenser. The feeders have drainage holes in the tubes and seed trays. They work well, but only if you clean the feeders regularly.

Every so often run the Droll Yankee through your dish-washer—it will come out intact and clean. Between fillings you must shake out the seeds and shells that accumulate under the bottom of the feeding portals.

These sunflower tubes have but two design flaws: seed is allowed to accumulate under the bottom portals, and the portal size is large enough for smaller birds to get trapped in them.

Dr. Barton Gershen of Gaithersburg, Maryland, has observed greedy finches getting caught in the bottom feeding portals while going after the very last seed. The company knows about this problem and is working to solve it. As with other feeders, you can avoid this by not letting a feeder go empty.

The Droll Yankee arrives with a three-year unconditional guarantee (yes, it's even covered against squirrel damage). The Droll Yankee guarantee is one of the best in the business.

The Droll Yankee line includes poles, seed trays, pole baffles, and hanging baffles.

The Droll Yankee A-6 Tube Feeder

Droll Yankee Thistle Feeder

This relatively expensive feeder is virtually indestructible. Heidi has one that's about twenty years old. The only sign of age is the clouded plastic.

Droll Yankee has solved the seed-below-the-bottom-of-the-feeding-portal problem with an inverted-V insert. The feeder is armored against squirrel attacks.

The only improvement would be optional short perches to help deter the house finches.

Super Silo Feeder

The Super Silo is the top-of-the-line model from the Hyde Company. The exterior—the parts subjected to the elements and squirrels—is made of durable Lexan and metal. The cap, feeding portals, and perches are metal.

The tube interior has an "even flow" tube that helps ensure a steady spill of seed, so each of the feeding portals has seed. But this inner tube is nearly impossible to clean and likely to break. The other problem with the Super Silo is the plastic sleeves on the metal perches. It takes about a season for them to deteriorate. Don't bother replacing them. They're totally unnecessary.

The Super Silo is dishwasher safe. Be sure to shake out any residual seed or shells between fillings. The Super Silo could also use an inverted-V wedge so seed doesn't sit below the feeding portals.

The Super Silo holds up to six pounds of sunflower seed and has nine feeding portals, which accommodate a lot of birds. Various accessories are available from Hyde including baffles, trays, and poles.

Gemini Feeder

The Gemini is a good tube feeder, slightly more elaborate than the basic tube feeder. It consists of two separate tubes that can be filled with different seeds, although we recommend filling both with the same seed. Instead of the typical plastic or metal top, the Gemini has a wooden roof, making it slightly more attractive than many other tube feeders. The Gemini holds three quarts of seed and has four perches.

The Gemini Feeder

The Droll Yankee Thistle Feeder

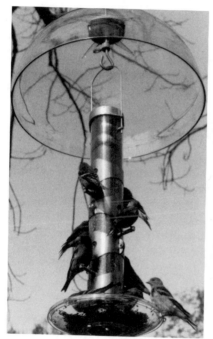

The Gemini Twin Tube Feeder

Gemini Twin Tube Feeder

The Twin Tube feeder is a smaller, uglier cousin of the Gemini. It holds two quarts of seed and can be hung or mounted on a pole. The seed compartments can be removed for cleaning—a real plus.

Distlefink Thistle Feeder

This inexpensive acrylic feeder comes with an aluminum cap and base, and green wooden perches. The wood perches disintegrate, are readily eaten by squirrels, and can become filled with bacteria. It will last a couple of years of hard use. It holds a couple pounds of thistle.

Aspects Twin Tube Feeders

The Aspects Company manufactures three attractive Twin Tube feeders, one- or two-quart capacity clear plastic feeders with aluminum trim and a three-quart plastic feeder with gray cedar trim. None is squirrel proof. All three can be post mounted and are easy to clean.

If you're tempted, use hulled sunflower and black-oil sunflower. Don't use a mix or millet in a tube feeder.

K-Feeders

The K-Feeder Company manufactures a line of moderately priced, good-quality tube feeders for sunflower or thistle seed. Don't use their seed trays, since they're way too deep and when it rains they clog up with shells and bird droppings.

Vari-Crafts Sunflower and Thistle Feeders

These nice-looking sunflower and thistle tubes are made of PVC pipe. There aren't many tube feeders that you can say look just as good as old milk bottles. The birds, of course, don't care two hoots about what a feeder looks like, but if you do, then these feeders are a good choice. The major differences between these feeders are the kind of seed they hold and size: The VCT-1, which holds one quart of seed, works with thistle seed only; the VCM-2, a two-quart feeder, is for sunflower. These are well-designed, sturdy hanging feeders, but they are not squirrel proof.

Nelson Pic-A-Seed Feeder

The Pic-A-Seed is a ready-to-go niger thistle feeder manufactured by Nelson Products. It's a hanging tube feeder that comes with everything you need to start feeding birds. All you have to do is open the top, remove and attach the hanging bracket (takes five or six seconds), then attach perches (another six seconds), and you're ready to go. It's hard to find an easier feeder to set up and use.

The Pic-A-Seed has all the benefits and limitations of hanging feeders (see other reviews). To its advantage, it has a "convertible feed flow," which lets you fill it with sunflower seed after the thistle is gone, so you're not stuck with having to buy expensive thistle in the hope of attracting goldfinches when all you actually get are house finches. (Keep in mind that if you fill the Pic-A-Seed with sunflower seed, only birds that feed at small perches will dine at this feeder.) Unfortunately, the Pic-A-Seed doesn't have a seed-catcher tray or any way of attaching a baffle on top.

The Pic-A-Seed holds about ten ounces of seed.

Artline Feeders

The Gas Lamp is a no-frills feeder from the Artline Company. Nothing elaborate; just a feeder that fills those birdies' tummies. Although we don't give prices in this book, the Gas Lamp is well priced for what you get.

The Gas Lamp holds a few pounds of seed. It's filled through a port on top. A plastic roof keeps rain off the seed, and a tray on the bottom doubles as a seed-catcher and feeding platform.

The Gas Lamp isn't squirrel resistant, but it's not designed to last long anyway. Because the Gas Lamp's plastic case is transparent, birds flock to it right away; not two minutes after we set up a tester in the yard, a tufted titmouse was nibbling at the hulled sunflower seed inside. The Gas Lamp works best with hulled sunflower or black-oil sunflower seed. It can be hung from a tree or mounted on a pole. If you place it on a pole and put a baffle beneath, you

The Artline Gass Lamp Feeder

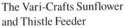

The Vari-Crafts Sunflower and Thistle Feeder

run a better chance of keeping squirrels away. Artline also manufactures a Coach Lamp feeder that is similar to the Gas Lamp in all regards except for shape.

Soda Bottle Birdfeeder

Even if price weren't a consideration, the Soda Bottle feeder would be one of the best around. It happens to be inexpensive, but it's also brilliant, and, believe it or not, reasonably squirrel resistant. The main drawback is that it looks like, well, a soda bottle. But the birds don't seem to mind.

A soda bottle birdfeeder

If you don't regularly drink soda, check with your neighbors who have kids. Buy them a treat in the two- or three-liter size. If you have problems justifying buying a plastic bottle, just think of using the soda bottle as recycling.

Another virtue of the Soda Bottle feeder is that you never have to clean it; when it gets icky, just put it in its final resting place. The feeder can be refilled a dozen or more times before it becomes dirty or chewed on by squirrels. To turn an ordinary bottle into a birdfeeder, simply attach the metal hanger to what was formerly the bottom of the bottle (and which is now the top of the feeder), and attach by twisting the metal screw adapter to what has become the bottom of the feeder. The metal screw adapter acts as the seed regulator and platform where birds can eat. Because soda bottles have a narrow mouth, filling the feeder requires a funnel-type scoop.

The seed is easily visible from all sides, so you'll attract a wide variety of species. A fair amount of spillage will bring cardinals, mourning doves, and juncos to the ground below the feeder. The feeder can be filled with sunflower seed, hulled sunflower, or peanut hearts. Finch Choice, a processed sunflower seed chopped into thistle-sized bits, seems to work best in the two-liter size.

The elongated shape of the bottle somehow prevents squirrels from gorging themselves. They manage to get some food, then slip off and have to start all over again. The feeder's shape also keeps the seed dry.

Four perches extend out from the three-liter screw adapter, so four birds can share the feeder. When we tested our Soda Bottle feeder, a chickadee appeared in five minutes.

Because you're likely to dispose of the feeder before it needs cleaning, because birds can't get inside, and because it has drainage holes, this is a very safe feeder.

Fadco Geometric Feeders

After a while, there's not a whole lot of innovation that can go into designing a birdfeeder. There are round feeders, rectangular feeders, square feeders, cylindrical feeders—what other shapes are left?

The Fadco Geometric Feeder

Fadco came up with inexpensive hexagonal thistle and sunflower feeders with six up and down feeding stations. So what's so great about that? The hexagonal design helps keep the seed dry, and allows you to see just about all the birds on the feeder.

The other advantage of this feeder is that it's filled from the bottom. That pushes old seed to the top where, unless it's spoiled, it's likely to be eaten.

The disadvantage of the sunflower feeder is that there's no interior baffle on the feeding portal to keep seed from spilling out. That's not as much a problem with the Fadco thistle feeders because the holes are so small.

Fadco Tube Sunflower and Thistle Feeders

Fadco feeders are inexpensive "starter" feeders. The tubes are made of butyrate plastic; the metal parts are made of steel and are coated with zinc for protection against rain. They should last about five years unless squirrels get to them, in which case they will last about five minutes.

EZ Fill Thistle Feeder

For thistle feeders, the EZ Fill has a large capacity. Its oversized top helps keep moisture off; however, the baffle isn't large enough to prevent squirrels from attacking the feeder. But the good news is that squirrels aren't all that crazy about thistle. However (and there's always a however with squirrels), they will chew through this feeder if they feel a need to.

Dartmouth Thistle Sock

Another convenient way to dispense thistle is through a thistle sock. The open mesh is large enough to enable finches to pull seed through the nylon but small enough to prevent thistle from spilling out on its own accord. A dozen birds can eat from the Thistle Sock at the same time. The sock is easily soiled, so you probably won't want to use it too many times before throwing it away.

Heath Vertical Perch Finch Feeder

These attractive tube feeders give finches several vantage points from which to eat thistle. They have a relatively large capacity and are easy to fill.

Creatively Designed Products Feeder

This ceramic feeder can hold either thistle or sunflower seeds. It's sturdy and attractive. The tray can become saturated with bird droppings, so it's advisable to clean it regularly.

Carruth Studio Kitty Feeder

We love it! Perhaps it's not such a good idea to get birds to associate cats with food (because the other way around is certainly true), but the Kitty Feeder helps make birdfeeding fun. The Carruth Kitty Feeder holds two cups of sunflower, safflower, or hulled sunflower seed.

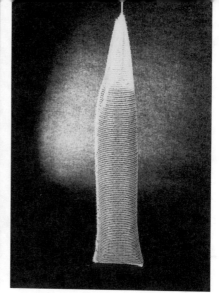

The EZ Fill Thistle Feeder   The Dartmouth Thistle Sock

Opus Fly-Thru Terra-Cotta Feeder

This semiplatform feeder can attract a variety of birds, depending on how high you place it and what kind of seed you fill it with. Although its design doesn't shelter the seed from a heavy rain, seed will stay dry during a slight to moderate rain. To fill the Fly-Thru, just pour seed in. Because birds are going to defecate on the seed, you should clean the feeder between fillings. Hose it down every time you fill it, and give the feeder a thorough washing once a month.

Droll Yankee X-1 Seed Saver Birdfeeder

The X-1 lets you adjust the space between the seed tray and baffle to squeeze out large birds such as blue jays, and help prevent squirrels from gaining access. But watch that squirrels can't get their little paws inside, or they will shake the feeder to spill seed onto the ground.

Birds can eat from all sides of the X-1. The feeder also enables you to view birds from all sides. Because this is a bowl-like feeder,

Heath Vertical Perch Finch Feeders

A ceramic feeder by Creatively Designed Products

The Opus Fly-Thru Terra-Cotta Feeder

The Carruth Studio Kitty Feeder

34

birds will not restrict themselves to eating from the rim of the tray. As a result, droppings accumulate on the seed, so wash the feeder regularly.

Seed vanishes from this feeder faster than you can fill it.

Restrictive Feeders

Restrictive feeders are designed to prevent certain species from getting into the feeder. They accomplish this by taking advantage of different birds' sizes and weights.

But before you go out and buy a new restrictive feeder, take a look at the feeders you've got, because you may be able to modify your feeder to make it more restrictive. If you have a tube feeder, a few simple changes such as shortening or removing the perches can eliminate visits from unwanted birds. Remember, seed selection may help too.

Select-A-Bird Feeder

Move over Captain Kirk. If you've longed for a birdfeeder that lets you do more than fill the feeder and watch—that lets you fiddle and tinker and plan and play—this is for you. The Select-A-Bird is based on two separate counterweights that control the leverage needed to open the "door" to the feeder. By turning the weights in the same way you would adjust a doctor's scale, you can vary the tension so that it opens only for the desired birds.

The feeder is normally in the closed position, with the opening on the door above the opening on the feeder. When the feeder hole on the door and the hole on the feeder are aligned, a bird can eat away. If a heavy bird lands on the perch, the opening on the door drops below the opening on the feeder; when a light bird lands, the opening on the door doesn't go down at all.

In practice, using the Select-A-Bird feeder isn't all that difficult. The feeder comes preadjusted for a cardinal's weight and setting up the feeder takes only about a minute.

The Select-A-Bird is an exciting feeder! Imagine, you can "dial out" house sparrows, finches, starlings, or even the dread pigeon.

The Droll Yankee X-1 Seed Saver Feeder   The Select-A-Bird Feeder

Adjusting the feeder for a particular bird takes some time. The difference in weight between a downy woodpecker and house sparrow is only four grams, so you may have to practice before you can set the weights to the desired amount.

The Select-A-Bird works on the principle that—unlike humans, who vary in dimension from very thin to Volkswagen-size—all birds of the same species weigh about the same. There are no fatsos in the bird world. But as the Select-A-Bird's manual points out, the weight of some species varies by season and region—this may give some trouble in "dialing" a bird.

The Select-A-Bird feeder can be pole mounted or hung from a tree. Pole mounting is the preferred method because, with a baffle beneath the feeder, the Select-A-Bird becomes virtually squirrel proof. Even if a squirrel gets to the feeder, its weight keeps the opening shut. The occasional extra-smart squirrel can figure out how to maneuver the two openings so that they are aligned, but— what the heck—any squirrel that can figure out counterweights and align holes deserves a little seed.

To fill a pole-mounted Select-A-Bird, just lift the top and pour in the seed.

Hanging the feeder presents a couple of problems. First, hanging feeders generally are easier for squirrels to break into, and the Select-A-Bird is no exception. Even with a baffle top, squirrels can break in. But the good news is that while hanging upside down (the way they have to eat from a hanging feeder), they can't consume that much. The other problem is that to refill the Select-A-Bird as a hanging feeder, you have to take it down before you can lift the top. The bracket that supports the Select-A-Bird also keeps the top in place. On the plus side, when it hangs you can place a baffle on top to help keep the Select-A-Bird dry in foul weather.

The Select-A-Bird holds only a quart of seed at a time. You can fill it with sunflower, safflower, or peanut kernels.

The Select-A-Bird's manual is about the most interesting we've seen. It comes with a list of weights for thirty-two birds and separate instructions on adjusting the feeder for cardinals, grosbeaks, extra-light birds such as chickadees, house sparrows (why you'd want to do that is another question), and goldfinches. The manual also gives the weights of various coins and a coin envelope that fits on the perch, so you can check the exact weight to open the door.

We don't recommend using the Select-A-Bird as your only feeder, because it will limit the kinds of birds attracted to your yard.

Hyde Tip Toe Feeder

The Hyde Company manufactures a redwood house feeder (with a pole) that operates on the same principle as the Select-A-Bird feeder. The Tip Toe Feeder is designed to keep large birds off your feeder. You set the flimsy adjustable counterweighted feeding perch and fill the feeder via a small hole in the roof.

You'll have to add a baffle to the pole to protect it from squirrels.

Duncraft Spinning Satellite Feeder

The Satellite Feeder by Duncraft has plenty of problems that make it undesirable. With that opening line, you'd think that our next sentence would be something like, "The Satellite is probably a better

The Duncraft Spinning Satellite Feeder

hockey puck than birdfeeder." But the Satellite is one of the most fun feeders available, if you're willing to keep it full of seed.

The Satellite is cute. It's even attractive. It's petite, and it doesn't stand out in your yard like some withering monument.

Now the bad news. The Satellite can only hold about a cup of sunflower seed. Only one clinging bird can eat out of it at a time. Refilling it is about as much fun as changing the oil in your car.

With a baffle, the seed inside is guaranteed to stay dry. Made of sparkling clear acrylic, it's easy pickins' for a squirrel. But because it's so small, the smarter squirrels may pursue bigger fish, as it were, and leave the Satellite alone. The dumber squirrels will attack the Satellite, and demolish it in a heartbeat. You can fill the Satellite with sunflower seed or hulled sunflower seed. Therein lies the most serious problem of all. You must keep the feeder full, or you will soon discover that this feeder can be lethal. Why? Because the hole the little chickadees cling to is just big enough for them to go into to get that last seed sitting at the back. Once they get inside, that sparkling clear acrylic confuses them. They can't figure how to get out.

Duncraft Cling-a-Wing Feeder

Duncraft's Cling-a-Wing has many of the same virtues and disadvantages as the Spinning Satellite. It doesn't hold much seed and is hard to fill. On the other hand, this feeder is cute as a button. And the birds think so, too.

The Duncraft Cling-a-Wing Feeder

Noel Restrictive Wire Feeder

If you don't mind the looks of yellow plastic and green vinyl-coated wire, and you want to feed only chickadees, titmice, and finches, Noel's Restrictive Wire Feeder is for you. The wire mesh is small enough to keep larger birds out.

Don't expect this feeder to be squirrel proof. The plastic top is easy chewing.

The restrictive Wire Feeder holds only a quart or so of sunflower seed, but seed in the center tube is protected from the elements. You will need a funnel to fill it.

Droll Yankee Jay Proof Feeder

If you don't like blue jays, Droll Yankee made this feeder for you. Instead of just telling you to take the perches off their A-6 and B-7 feeders, they made a new feeder with springs instead of solid metal perches. The same chickadees, titmice, and finches that use the spring perches on the jay-proof feeder will also visit your A-6 without perches. How do they do it? They just cling to the metal feeding portals.

Like all Droll Yankee feeders, this one is made of polycarbonate and comes with a three-year unconditional guarantee.

Squirrel-Proof Feeders

K-Feeder Ultimate

This triple-tube ultimate feeder and its smaller cousin, the Carousel, are touted by the manufacturer as being squirrel proof. In fact, the K-Feeder promotional material says the "squirrel guard, metal baffles, aluminum perches and reinforcing make this feeder *as squirrel-proof as possible* [italics added]." Unfortunately, squirrels can't read that information. They regularly eat the baffle and the tubes. They also eat the perches on the Carousel.

These feeders look great in the photos on the packaging. If you hang them where a squirrel can get even close to the baffle, it's just a matter of time. Your feeder will be destroyed.

The only other problem with the Ultimate and the Carousel is that the manufacturer wants you to "dispense sunflower, wild bird mixes, and thistle seed independently and simultaneously." If you take them at their word, you'll get a busy sunflower tube, then an emptied mixed seed tube with a mess piled in the tray, and a tube of untouched thistle, which is likely to spoil.

Hyde Squirrel's Dilemma

Only a very dumb squirrel would consider this feeder a dilemma, and then only for a few hours. The feeder features a twelve-station styrene tube surrounded by green vinyl-coated fox wire. Hyde says, "the birds can access the seed through the wire, but the squirrels' access is limited to an occasional pawful—they cannot chew on the feeder or get their heads through the wire." The squirrels we know had no trouble getting their heads through the wire and the styrene tube.

Noel Squirrel-Less Sunflower Feeder

Noel's Squirrel-less Sunflower Feeder is made of an inexpensive plastic tube with twelve feeding portals encased in vinyl-coated wire. Like the Squirrel's Dilemma, the object here is to keep the squirrels' mouths off the tube. Noel's succeeds.

Squirrels will get to this feeder, but the tube is far enough from the wire casing to let them get only an occasional pawful. A unique inner-tube skirt over the feeding portals helps minimize spillage. It comes with a three-year warranty.

The K-Feeder Ultimate

The Hyde Squirrel's Dilemma

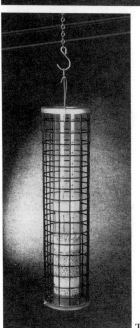

The Noel Squirrel-less Sunflower Feeder

Noel Squirrel-Proof Thistle Feeder

Like its cousin the Squirrel-less Sunflower Feeder, this feeder keeps squirrels from chewing on thistle. It comes with sixteen feeding portals and holds about three pounds of seed.

If you put Finch Choice in it, expect to cash in on your warranty. Squirrels apparently are crazed by the sight of Finch Choice, and virtually consume even the wire mesh. However, there is an advantage to using Finch Choice in this feeder. You'll see an incredible variety of birds: red-bellied woodpeckers, Carolina wrens, downy and hairy woodpeckers, chickadees, titmice and nuthatches, and, yes, goldfinches.

GSP Feeder

MH Industries GSP (Guaranteed Squirrel-Proof) Feeder is one of the most written-about feeders. Designed by a Connecticut chemist, Stephen Clarke, the GSP quickly earned a patent and a place in the U.S. Patent Office's annual inventors' exhibition. The GSP, which is nearly 100 percent squirrel proof, works on a simple principle: birds fly, but squirrels can't. Only critters that can fly up and into the GSP's feeding hollow can get at the seed.

The GSP holds over one and a half gallons of seed—either sunflower or hulled sunflower seed. The seed is dispensed along a cavity between two plastic walls into two troughs. Birds can perch on either of the two troughs. Although not mentioned in the instructions, you can hang a suet basket from the inside nut, so the GSP will also attract woodpeckers. Starlings aren't crazy about this suet arrangement and are likely to avoid the feeder.

The major drawback of the GSP is that the plastic will become cloudy and dirty over time, obscuring your view of the birds. Also, the GSP is fragile: if it lands on cement, it's likely to break.

Wildlife Products Squirrel-Proof Sunflower Feeder

What happens when you make a tube from stainless-steel wire mesh and add a metal roof and tray? Add black-oil sunflower seed and you get Wildlife Products' Squirrel-Proof Sunflower Feeder. It holds

The MH Industries GSP Feeder

The Arthur C. Brown Audubon
Squirrel-Proof Feeder

about ten pounds of seed and offers clinging birds over 240 square inches of feeding area.

It's nowhere as beautiful as a wooden feeder, but squirrels can't destroy it, and it won't rust. If you absolutely have to hang your feeder in a tree, and don't mind if the squirrels get to it once in a while, this is your feeder.

Arthur C. Brown Audubon Squirrel-Proof Feeders

The Arthur C. Brown Company manufactures two large cylindrical aluminum and plastic feeders they call the Audubon Squirrel-Proof Feeders. The pole-mounted feeder holds about a gallon of sunflower seed and comes with a three-section pole. Squirrels climb up the pole and get confused by the stove-pipe green aluminum baffle.

The hanging version has the green stove pipe incorporated into the top of the cylinder, doubling the seed capacity. Squirrels try to climb down the cylinder and slip off the additional Lexan collar that covers the perches.

These feeders cater to small birds. The perches are not large enough for cardinals and doves. You must not put these feeders within a squirrel's lateral leaping range. They will amaze you by grabbing hold of the tiny perches and demolishing them. The good news is that all parts of the feeder are replaceable, but not always under warranty.

Because these feeders have such a large capacity, regular monthly cleaning is needed to minimize seed spoilage.

Graham Carlson Hylarious Feeder

The Graham Carlson Company invented an odd-looking sheet-metal box with an open front covered by a hood connected to a perch, which in turn is connected to a weighted counterbalance on the back of the box. Understand?

When birds come to the perch, they weigh too little to shut the hood. Not so with squirrels. It is just hilarious to watch the squirrels try just about everything to get into the feeder.

For years the Graham Carlson Company was the only place you could buy one of these Hylarious feeders. That was until their patent ran out. Now you can get clones (the Eliminator, Squirrel Buster, Foiler—you get the idea) from several manufacturers. All but one shares the same problems as the original version: problem drainage (bottom rusts, seed rots); small feeding surfaces; in icy weather the back counterbalance freezes the feeder hoppers in the open position; the door latches are difficult to open (even for humans).

The Graham Carlson Company now offers a "bottom baffle" to facilitate seed flow and drainage, which can be retrofitted. All you need is a piece of plastic to wedge inside, tilted forward.

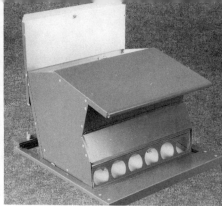

The Graham Carlson Hylarious Feeder   The Nelson Products Foiler

Nelson Products Foiler

The Foiler is one of several metal counterbalance feeders that appeared on the market after the Hylarious patent expired.

As these types of feeders go, the Foiler performs its function okay. But it has some important deficiencies. First, it's made of sheet metal with sharp edges; a sluggish bird might be decapitated if its head gets caught against one of these edges. The Foiler has no drainage holes, which means rust and moldy seed can be problems.

Looker Steel Squirrel-Proof Feeder (SSP)

Looker Products' Steel Squirrel-Proof Feeder is the fortress of bird feeders. As they say, "There ain't no squirrels that are gonna get in the SSP." If you want to feed cardinals and other birds, and don't want any sunflower to go to the squirrels, this is the feeder for you.

The SSP has attributes besides being stalwartly squirrel resistant. It has a large capacity—about five pounds. If you fill the feeder with black-oil sunflower seed, you'll get cardinals, jays, doves, chickadees, finches, and titmice.

The Steel Squirrel-Proof Feeder is durable. Bill had fastened the SSP to a pole with glue. After a couple of winters the glue wore out and the feeder dropped five feet onto cement. Then it fell again. Even after falling twice, the Steel Squirrel-Proof Feeder was in perfect working order. (Next time he used epoxy.)

The Steel Squirrel-Proof Feeder is a spring-loaded platform feeder. Birds stand on the platform and feast on the seed in front of them. As many as seven birds can eat at the same time. While Lookers insists on gluing wood to the steel platform, it's not necessary and can be unhealthy for the birds. When the squirrels chew it off, don't get upset. Just don't replace it.

But when a squirrel tries to get onto the platform, its weight causes the platform to move down, pulling a metal door down with it that blocks access to the seed. No lunch for that squirrel! Thin, smart squirrels have learned, however, that by moving as far forward as possible and shifting their weight they can cause the platform to move up and the door to open. You can counter this move by adjusting the SSP's springs to the lightest setting. The SSP has several weight settings. In some instances a squirrel or two may be able to get at the seed even at the lightest setting. If this happens just stretch the spring.

You can adjust the Steel Squirrel-Proof Feeder so that it thwarts starlings and other large birds—or prevents more than three birds from eating at the same time.

The SSP is a relatively safe feeder. Two of the major problems that birds face with feeders—becoming trapped inside and eating wet, moldy seed—are not as likely to happen with the Steel Squirrel-Proof Feeder. The top goes around the sides entirely and the front "roof" extends several inches over the feeding platform. We've yet to see an SSP get wet inside even during the most horrendous rain—you know, one of those rains that goes horizontally and downward at the same time.

It's just about the easiest feeder on the market to fill. Simply unsnap the back latch, lift the hinged top, and fill 'er up! You can use a scoop or a seed silo, or even pour the seed from a bag right into the feeder.

The Steel Squirrel-Proof Feeder has to be mounted on a pole; it's not designed to be hung. You can buy a pole kit, but it's just as easy, and much less expensive, to have the hardware store cut you a 5-foot 2 by 3 of pressure-treated lumber. For best results, screw the feeder base to the pole.

The SSP should last for years. The paint may chip after a handful of winters. If that's a problem, or if you happen not to like its original color (green), use Rustoleum to paint over it.

Heath Animated Feeder

The Animated Feeder looks great in the Heath Company catalog. When you put it in your yard, it looks great for a couple of hours, until it gets jammed and the squirrels eat through the plastic top.

Here's how it's supposed to work. A protective metal cone covers the cylindrical plastic seed hopper. The cone is connected to the feeding perch and controlled by a spring clip attached to the pole. Squirrels and large birds are supposed to grab the feeding perch and their weight pulls the metal cone down, shutting off the seed supply.

It holds about a cup of seed and is likely to drive you, not the squirrels, crazy.

Mandarin Feeder

Overall, the Mandarin is one of the best hanging plastic feeders on the market, with only a couple of flaws, which we'll get to later. In short, it's highly squirrel proof, has a large seed capacity, is easy to fill, has high bird visibility, is durable, and is easy to hang.

The Mandarin's oriental-hat design helps keep seed dry. The "hat" is a built-in baffle, which helps keep rain, snow, and falling leaves out of the seed; moisture simply spills onto the ground. The Mandarin has no drainage holes so you would be wise to drill a few in the bottom.

The steepness of the hat and fact that it overhangs the side of the feeder by several inches prevents most squirrels from getting at the seed. This is not to say that they won't try. Squirrels love to wrap their back claws around the Mandarin's center chain and try to reach over the baffle. It's fun to watch if you also enjoy squirrel watching; it's a bit of a problem if you don't like squirrels, because when a squirrel is on the feeder, birds tend to stay away.

47

The Looker Products Steel Squirrel-Proof Feeder

The Mandarin Feeder

Now occasionally an extra-long squirrel is going to be able to reach over as far as the perches. What will he do when he reaches them? What all squirrels do when they encounter a barrier: he'll eat the perches. You can eliminate this problem by removing the perches altogether. Most of the birds that are attracted to the Mandarin don't need those perches. Taking them away also solves another occasional problem. Depending on how you hang your Mandarin, some agile squirrels may be able to leap laterally and grab on to a perch. And to give the Mandarin that final anti-squirrel touch, place a soup can through the chain and over the top, which prevents squirrels from chewing through around the top washer.

You can fill the Mandarin with sunflower seed, hulled sunflower seed, or peanut kernels. Its five-pound capacity means that you're not going to have to run out every day—or even every other day. Depending on how hungry the birds in your neighborhood are, you may be able to get away with refilling the Mandarin once every week or ten days. During the cold winter months or one of those rains that seem to last for days, that's a blessing. The Mandarin is translucent acrylic, and as a result you can determine from a distance whether the feeder has run out of seed.

The Mandarin attracts small birds capable of holding on to the small perches: finches, sparrows, chickadees, tufted titmice, starlings, nuthatches, even downy woodpeckers will visit the Mandarin when they're hungry. Starlings, which happen to love the Mandarin, tend to make a real mess (and eat a lot, but that's more the fault of starlings than the Mandarin). Consequently, other birds such as cardinals, mourning doves, and juncos hang around under the Mandarin.

You'll be able to see birds eating from three sides. If your feeder doesn't sway too much (and spill seed), you might want to consider blocking off the feeding hole on the side opposite your living room window (or wherever).

Now for the flaws. First, some feeder owners have reported that when the Mandarin becomes low on seed, chickadees push themselves inside the too-large feeding portals to get at the remaining seed, where they become trapped. There are two ways to prevent this. First, make sure that the Mandarin is never low on seed. When you go away, take the Mandarin down and put up another feeder in its place. Or simply cover the holes if you don't think you'll get to your feeder for a while. Second, halve the entrance by gluing a dowel over the feeding hole. This will divide it into two smaller holes that a chickadee can't enter.

The Mandarin should last several seasons, although the plastic will become cloudy over time. It's pretty durable and will survive prolonged squirrel attacks. As with all feeders, be sure to clean it regularly.

Nelson Fortress Feeder

Another Nelson Products feeder, the Fortress receives above-average ratings in most categories. It holds a substantial amount of seed—several pounds. It lets up to ten birds eat at one time, depending on how they get along. The Fortress keeps the rain out and provides drainage when a heavy rain does get the seed wet. Its sturdy, metal construction and sloping sides provide a measure of anti-squirrel capabilities. The Fortress isn't squirrel proof, but squirrels won't find this feeder their restaurant of choice.

The main sides of the Fortress are constructed of clear plastic, so that it's easy to tell when this feeder is running out of seed. (Because much of the Fortress' surface area is clear, birds can easily spot the seed, too.) To fill, twist the locking nut that secures the top in place, tilt the top open on its hinge, and pour. One of the nicer attributes of the Fortress is that you can refill it with one hand; unlike many feeders, you don't have to hold something open while putting in seed.

Fill the Fortress with black-oil sunflower seed, hulled sunflower seed, safflower seed, or peanut kernels.

The Fortress comes with its own pole. Set-up takes less than two minutes.

Duncraft Estate Feeder

We don't know why Duncraft decided to call this pole feeder the Estate Feeder, because we've never seen anything resembling it on any estate we've been to. But on the other hand, it's a great name.

Sunflower seeds, hulled sunflower seeds, and peanuts work best in this feeder, but you can also fill it with safflower seed to discourage squirrels.

The Estate Feeder holds about two quarts of sunflower nearly 6 feet off the ground. This height makes the squirrels work for their meal. The seed sits in a plastic bowl sandwiched between two baffles, which ought to protect your feeder from squirrels, torrential rain, and tennis balls gone astray.

Two potential problems with the Estate Feeder—as with all bowl feeders—are drainage and bird droppings. If rain does get in, the bowl shape does not permit any drainage, so seed may get moldy. Inspect the feeder regularly to avoid this problem. You might also consider drilling a few small holes in the bottom of the feeder. The best solution to the bird droppings problem is to clean your feeder regularly; unfortunately, wild birds cannot be litter trained. Even if you don't own a bowl-shaped feeder like the Estate Feeder, cleaning your feeder once a month is a good idea.

Droll Yankee Big Top Feeder

You'll probably like the Big Top. It looks great. It has such a great name. It works great, if you don't let the birds sit in the seed and you don't expect the squirrels to chew through the eight plastic feeding portals below.

The Big Top combines the best of several different attributes. It looks squirrel proof. It holds a large amount of seed—three quarts in all. It has drainage ports (the same ones the birds eat out of) to eliminate excess moisture. The Big Top comes with a giant baffle that keeps rain off and prevents most squirrels from getting inside. You can adjust the space between the seed bowl and the baffle to (1) make it more difficult for the birds to defecate on the seed and (2) make it impossible for large birds to reach the food. The Big Top also can be filled with black-oil sunflower seed, hulled sunflower seed, or peanut kernels.

There's an eyelet knob at the bottom of the Big Top that lets you adjust the flow of seed into the lower bowl. The manufacturer recommends that you attach a suet bell to the eyelet and use the Big Top to attract woodpeckers as well. The problem is that your suet is bound to get contaminated by bird droppings, since it sits below the feeding portals. Not a good strategy.

Finally, the Big Top is easy to install and easy to fill. Droll Yankee has kept in mind the human quotient. (Feeders that are hard to fill end up becoming not unlike abandoned cars.)

The Big Top is what we call a dual bowl feeder: a large bowl—a rain shield and squirrel baffle—is placed on top of a smaller bowl. All other things being equal, the larger the top bowl is relative to the bottom bowl, the better the feeder works. In the case of the Big Top, the feeder has a very big top. The Squirrel Baffle Bird Feeder and Dome Feeder are similar in design. There can be problems with this arrangement, however. You want to be able to vary the space

The Droll Yankee Big Top Feeder

between the two bowls *easily* to allow for changing squirrel conditions. The Big Top is among the few feeders that does that.

Both domes are made of the durable polycarbonate plastic. The more vulnerable feeding portals are too. Keep your warranty, as you may need to replace them.

Birds can eat from either the eight ports at the base of the feeder or from the top of the lower bowl. We don't recommend that you allow large birds to feed inside in the bowl.

The Big Top is exclusively a hanging feeder. To refill the feeder you can either pour seed directly into the lower bowl or remove the bowl to refill it. Having the bowl easily detachable from the baffle gives the Big Top another plus—you're more likely to clean it, reducing the risk of mold and bacteria contaminating the seed.

Karlsburg Fiesta Feeder

Let's put it this way. The Fiesta birdfeeder isn't going to win you any awards in a garden magazine. In fact, if your local zoning ordinances prohibit putting objects in your yard that resemble space ships (especially 1930s artists' renditions of space ships), you may not be able to use the Fiesta.

Extraterrestrial problems aside, the Fiesta is a marvelous feeder. First it's as squirrel proof as they come. (Squirrels, despite their limited intelligence, may actually be wary of coming too close to the Fiesta, lest they be carried away into the interstellar void.) The Fiesta's top, which doubles as a baffle, fits so snugly, completely, and securely over the roof of the feeder that there's no way a squirrel can squeeze inside or pull the top off.

The Fiesta can be mounted on a pole or hung from a tree. When pole mounted, the bottom baffle should prevent most squirrels from getting to the seed. (Most squirrels past the age of two months can figure out a way to get into any tree-hung feeder.) Because a few extra-agile, extra-hungry squirrels can get over the lower baffle, it's wise to put another baffle beneath the Fiesta or to grease the pole. But even if squirrels can get over the baffle, the seed opening is too small for them to get more than just a little seed at a time. The plastic roof and bottom baffle do present teething opportunities to squirrels, but while that may mar your Fiesta, it ought to take a long time before squirrels actually penetrate the feeder through these points. Needless to say, the squirrels aren't going to get through the galvanized steel of the Fiesta's body.

The Fiesta dispenses seed from 360 degrees. This is good news for the birds; they don't have to wait for an opening at a seed port, the avian equivalent of waiting for a bank teller. But this is also bad news for birdwatchers; at any given time you won't be able to see half the birds eating. But that's a small price to pay for making the birds happy.

The Karlsburg Fiesta Feeder

"Formidable" is the Fiesta's middle name. It's fairly impervious not only to squirrels but to the elements as well. The oversize top keeps rain and snow off the seed, and the seed silo not only keeps seed dry but drains away moisture. Because the space through which seed is dispensed is small, birds can't get trapped inside. In addition, bird droppings can't get on the seed inside, as they can with bowl feeders. The plastic feeding platform doesn't provide a breeding ground for disease, as wooden platforms do. It's a safe feeder for the birds.

You can fill the Fiesta with sunflower seed, hulled sunflower seed, safflower seed, or thistle seed. Because birds eat from a platform, cardinals like this feeder. The Fiesta holds about four to six quarts of seed, which is a good thing because filling the Fiesta is not fun. You have to either remove the entire feeder from the pole or unscrew the top and then find somebody who's at least 6 feet tall to refill it. Then you have to screw the top back on. Well, nothing's perfect. When you're refilling the Fiesta, you might as well clean it, too.

Window Feeders

One of the nicest things about birds is that an easy meal will make them overcome their fear of people. It may take some time, but some wild birds are easily tamed.

If you're patient—and you have strong arms—you can actually train them to come to your outstretched hand. But it's a lot easier to get them to discover and use feeders attached to your windows. In fact, they will even come inside the house (to an in-house window feeder) if you offer just the right food.

Which window feeder is right for you? It's not a simple decision, since there are dozens to choose from. Most are plastic; some are a combination of plastic and wood or metal.

When selecting a window feeder, the most important criteria is squirrels, followed by looks, seed capacity, the birds you want to attract, and finally price.

Even if you've seen only one squirrel in your yard, that squirrel will menace your feeder. Think long and hard about your backyard environment before you make the purchase. A window feeder may not be a wise idea if:

- You have to hang it near a tree (less than 10 feet away).
- Your house is wood or brick (they'll climb).
- The window is less than five feet from the ground (they'll jump).

Squirrels like to jump into window feeders from above. A few, like Droll Yankee's Winner, have baffles to thwart this.

You won't see many birds when the squirrels are eating your bird-seed. Bill Adler's book *Outwitting Squirrels* was, in large measure, inspired by a squirrel who liked to lie down and eat in Bill's rectangular window feeder. Worse still, once they get to a window feeder, squirrels are likely to destroy the feeder by eating the plastic, or by causing the feeder to fall to the ground.

On the plus side, squirrels can't climb glass, so if your window is large enough you may be automatically protected. If you have double-hung windows, and price is not a problem, take a look at the in-house window feeders. Designed to sit in an opened fifteen-, twenty-four- or twenty-seven-inch frame, these feeders are equipped with one-way mirrored glass to keep birds from seeing you. They are called in-house because part of the feeder extends into your house. Besides giving you a close-up view of the birds, in-house feeders make excellent television for cats.

Most window feeders are secured by suction cups. The more suction cups, the tighter the hold; and the larger the seed capacity of the feeder, the more you need a tight hold. The life expectancy of poorly secured window feeders is short. If you plan to put your feeder on a second-story window, consider one of sturdy polycarbonate or Lexan plastic, because it's not a matter of if, but *when* the feeder will hit the ground. After you've made your purchase and put your feeder on the window, be patient. Birds are not very bright (hence the term bird brain). It will take some time for them to recognize your window as a source of food.

You may hurry the process by putting some reflective kitchen foil or a big piece of paper behind the feeder. Often all it takes to attract a bird's attention is something out of the ordinary—a reflection or flash of light from your feeder will do. Once a single bird has found a feeder, that bird will tell dozens of others and within a day you'll be hosting a party.

You don't have to worry about birds crashing into your window. When birds smash into your window, it's because they see a reflection and think they're flying through the woods. A window feeder will break up that reflection.

Feeders with built-in reflective qualities are recent additions to the fast-growing window feeder market. Their one-way see-through mirror allows you to see the birds without their seeing you. All the birds see is their reflections.

As a category, window feeders have certain strengths and weaknesses. They are the perfect feeder for apartment dwellers because you simply attach them to a window. The birds come close to you and after a short while may even get used to seeing humans up close. Their drawbacks include a relatively small seed capacity. The suction cups just can't support much weight. And eventually the suction cups fail; most window feeders don't survive more than a year. If you want to use your window feeder after it falls, have replacement suction cups. If you live above the third floor or have brick beneath your window, reuse is not a viable option. Finally, you have to be a bit of a daredevil to attach the feeder to the outside of a window that's twelve stories above the ground. (Yes, birds will visit a feeder that high up.)

There are basically three kinds of window feeders: in-house feeders that bring the birds inside the house, windowsill feeders that attach on the windowsill outside, and suction-cup feeders that hold onto the glass. The first in-house window feeder was a plain glass aquarium mounted in a window. Now these feeders are made of plastic with one-way mirrored film on three sides and a wooden platform floor. Filled from the top, indoors, the slight downward tilt allows for water drainage. If you don't have a squirrel problem, feeders that screw onto a windowsill or deck railing are an attractive option. Covered with plastic, they keep the seed dry and restrict visitation to small birds such as chickadees, finches, and titmice.

Avia Inc. Aviarium In-House Feeder

The Aviarium was first on the market. This award-winning feeder is made of pine or mahogany. The optional rain shield keeps the seed dry. The optional quilted cover adds insulation in the winter.

With easy-to-follow instructions, the Aviarium is simple to install. The only drawback is filling it with seed, fruit, or suet. Unless you fill it from the outside, two small corked holes are your only access. A Heath funnel scoop makes the job easier, but it is still a hassle.

Arthur C. Brown In-House Viewmaster Feeder

The Viewmaster from Arthur C. Brown Company is made of pine and has a one-way mirrored film on plastic. With its large top portal, the Viewmaster is light-years more convenient to fill than any other in-house feeder. Alas, with the good comes the bad: unless you special-order a feeder with exact window dimensions, you almost need to be a carpenter to install it.

Once you get past the aggravation of installing the Viewmaster you'll appreciate the fact that you can fold up the hinged feeding platform and close the window when the feeder is not in use. It's also a distinct security advantage if you live in an urban area where the wildlife is the two-legged variety.

Opus Clear View Windowsill Feeder

Opus window platform feeders have a thick plastic roof covering a thin untreated pine floor and six wooden dowels spaced a couple of inches apart to keep large birds (cardinals, doves, and jays) off. Don't buy this windowsill feeder unless you're prepared to open your window to fill it. Think about how often you'll do this in the winter.

It's not squirrel proof, and has all the disadvantages of a platform feeder.

Hyde Bird Cafe Feeder

The Hyde Company manufactures the Bird Cafe, a redwood-stained pine windowsill feeder with a thin plasti-glass top. It can hold three pounds of seed. A little larger than the Clear View, it suffers from the same design flaws.

Droll Yankee Winner Feeder

The Winner is one of the best window feeders available. It has excellent weather protection and an adjustable baffle to keep large birds out. The Winner is supported by either two suction cups (when one fails, your feeder won't end up in little plastic pieces on the pavement), by a top-supporting window bracket, or by a bottom supporting window bracket.

The Winner can be filled with black-oil sunflower seed, hulled sunflower seed, peanut kernels, or raisins. It's fun to fill the Winner only with whole peanuts, which will attract blue jays. Squirrels, of course, have a difficult time climbing glass, so the Winner has built-in anti-squirrel protection.

The Winner has inadequate drainage and can become filled with rain water and bird droppings. Because it comes off its mountings easily (something that can't be said for all window feeders), it's fairly effortless to clean.

A small tray feeder with a canopy roof, with the right food, the Winner attracts mockingbirds and red-bellied woodpeckers as well as chickadees and titmice.

There are two major disadvantages to this feeder: birds may be frightened away by human movement in the house and the feeder holds only a couple of cups of seed. Also, there's no mirrored backing to the Winner.

Documentation is adequate. The Winner, constructed of Lexan, comes with a three-year warranty.

Duncraft Classic II Feeder

Duncraft's Classic II is a basic window feeder—nothing fancy. But it's easy to fill and clean. You can put in sunflower seeds, hulled sunflower seeds, shelled peanuts—or even whole peanuts, if you want to attract blue jays and an occasional titmouse. If you're careful about cleaning, you can even use the Classic II as a window birdbath.

Tweeter Peeper Gourmet Buffet Feeder

By preventing birds from seeing you, the mirrored back panel of the Gourmet Buffet by Tweeter Peeper Products solves the problem of birds being frightened away when they see you. But it doesn't solve another problem—seed capacity. The Buffet has two seed bins that together hold about a cup.

The Droll Yankee
Winner Feeder

The Duncraft Classic II Feeder

Like the Winner, the Buffet can be mounted on suction cups or on a sill bracket. Unlike the Winner, it's made of acrylic. And it will not survive falling from the window or a squirrel attack.

The documentation is somewhat unfinished; the folks from Tweeter Peeper want you to use thistle or millet in one bin and sunflower in the other. If you follow their advice, most of your small seed will end up on the ground under the feeder. Better to fill both bins with the same seed—sunflower.

Unfortunately, much of the advice the Tweeter Peeper people offer is anecdotal. Their brochure needs these corrections:

- Birds will not die in severe weather if you don't fill your Buffet.
- There is nothing "wrong" with feeding birds year-round. On the contrary, if you want to help the birds when they're most stressed, feed them during migration and in the summer.
- Contrary to what the documentation says, you can fill the feeder from inside your house but you have to open the window to get to it.
- Birds don't need proximity to trees and shrubs to feel secure enough to visit a feeder, but *squirrels* will appreciate the branches and bushes to climb on.
- Predators (cats and raccoons) aren't likely to scale the side of your house, but if you have wood or brick siding, squirrels will be there before you can say "Tweeter Peeper."
- Birds are not very bright. "Spreading seed on the ground in the area of the new feeder" is not likely to help them make the connection and look up. Try spreading seed on the top of the feeder.

The Tweeter Peeper comes with a two-year guarantee and a one-year guarantee for the mirrored finish.

Meta Birdfeeder

The Meta Birdfeeder solves the problems of seed capacity and "the birds can see you watching them at the window." The feeding area is covered with a one-way mirror. The unique funnel seed reservoir holds about three pounds of sunflower seed—a considerable amount. This expensive feeder is as close as you can get to perfect.

The Meta Birdfeeder is made of squirrel-proof Lexan plastic. Regardless of squirrel attacks, Meta is the only feeder with a lifetime warranty. If any component breaks, send it back to Meta and you'll get a replacement part, at no charge.

The Meta's snap-apart construction makes it easy to clean and run through a dishwasher. The large dowel perches make it easy for large birds including mockingbirds to visit. If you'd rather not put it on the window, just pop out the "magic window" panels and prop it on a pole.

The Meta Birdfeeder comes packed with wonderfully complete instructions as well as an Opus bird-identification chart. The only problem with the written material is Meta's claim that the feeder can accommodate more species because it has three separate perches.

Birds not of a feather do not always flock together. We've seen one mockingbird fight off all comers to keep this feeder to himself. Unfortunately, Meta recommends using several seeds in a feeder. Ignore the recommendation and stick to sunflower only.

Artline Window Bird Feeder

There are plenty of window birdfeeders to choose from, so manufacturers must find a way of making their feeders unique. Generally there are two ways of doing this: making the feeder cute or cuter.

Artline's Window Bird Feeder has all the good and bad aspects of a window feeder. Its capacity is small—only a few ounces. But it's inexpensive and cute. A thermometer faces inside so you can watch birds eat in amazement: "It's ten below zero and the cold doesn't seem to bother them at all!" If placed in the middle of a large window, squirrels shouldn't be able to touch it.

Many window feeders have a bracket that separates the feeder from the suction cup apparatus. This lets you lift the feeder from the window to refill it without having to take the suction cups off. Unfortunately, the Artline Window Bird Feeder is attached to the suction cups, so to refill it from the inside you have to remove the entire feeder. (Refilling it from the outside isn't a problem; just lift the top and pour in the seed.) Once you've gone through all the trouble of getting the darn thing to stick to the window, you don't want to have to remove it.

The Artline Window Bird Feeder   The Nelson Products Window Watch Feeder

The Artline Window Bird Feeder has two feeding stations. It attracts titmice, chickadees, finches, sparrows, and, once in a while, mockingbirds.

Nelson Window Watch Feeder

Manufactured by Nelson Products, the Window Watch is a transparent cylinder sandwiched between a wide brim top and smaller diameter seed-catcher/perching platform. The Window Watch attaches to a window to give you close-up viewing of birds. There's a thermometer on the bracket facing the window. It's easy to put together.

Like most window feeders, the Window Watch will eventually fall, especially because it can hold more seed than the typical window feeder. (One bit of advice we have to Nelson Products: a third suction cup on the bottom would make the Window Watch adhere more securely.) Until its ultimate drop to the ground, the feeder will attract a wide range of birds, including titmice, chickadees, cardinals, mourning doves, nuthatches, and mockingbirds, bringing them to within 3 inches of your window.

Setting up the Window Watch is a snap. The arm that holds the feeder mounts easily onto the suction-cup brackets; the feeder fits easily onto the notch at the end of the arm. And the feeder itself is put together by a swift twisting motion.

The bracket is see-through and has a thermometer—the latest trend in window feeders—that faces indoors. The Window Watch gives excellent visibility of birds. It's available in yellow or black.

The Window Watch contains what Nelson Products calls *Dial-A-Seed*, a mechanism that adjusts the flow of seed from stingy to generous. Adjusting the seed flow involves no more than turning the bottom part of the feeder.

Alas, the Window Watch is not easy to fill. Fortunately, it's easy to remove from the bracket, but once inside, taking the top off is a pain. First you have to remove the plastic anchoring pin; then you have to twist off the top, and reverse the process when you are finished.

The Window Watch works well with black-oil sunflower seed and sunflower hearts.

Aspects Window Feeders

The Aspects Company's window feeders share the same design components: a removable clear plastic cup held in a C-shape clear plastic frame, which shields the feed from rain and large birds. They come in three sizes. The Snack Bar has one tray. The two tray feeders are available in two styles, the Buffet with a plain plastic roof and the Chalet with a larger gray-stained cedar roof to accommodate larger birds. The Banquet measures 4 by 12 by 5 inches and holds three trays "for a varied feast or when birds arrive in flocks."

These feeders are cute but aggravating. Squirrels don't just chew them up, they seem to derive great pleasure from yanking the

Aspects Company window
feeders

removable feeding trays (and often the feeders themselves) to the ground. If a couple of doves take to the feeder, their weight alone is often enough to pull the suction cups loose. And as tempting as it may be, don't search for different seeds to put in the trays. Just use sunflower.

Hyde Window Vu Feeder

This clear plastic tube feeder has six feeding ports on three levels, each with a separate seed supply, thanks to Hyde's patented "even seed system." The even seed system is a series of interior baffles that distribute seed to each feeding station until all the seed is consumed.

All you have to do is fill it with sunflower and hook it to the polycarbonate hanging bracket that's held to the window suction cups. Filling it may be your biggest challenge. It's easy enough to remove from the window, but the cap is another problem altogether.

Squirrels may not be able to eat the bracket, but if they can get to the feeder they'll just smack it to the ground, where we guarantee it will readily break in two.

Opus Window Feeders

Opus makes two extremely inexpensive small plastic tube window feeders that hold a pound of sunflower or thistle. Each has a tray and is held to the window with two sturdy suction cups. They work fine if the squirrels don't get to them.

Opus also makes the smallest window feeder you'll ever see. Smaller than your hand, this little plastic square holds less than a handful of sunflower seed. Chickadees and titmice will visit this feeder. But in order to keep them happy, you'll have to visit it just about as often to keep it full.

Looker Window Feeders

The same people who bring you the Steel Squirrel-Proof Feeder make window feeders, too. Both the Twin Hopper and the Center Hopper are clear Plexiglas rectangular boxes. They're filled from the top, at the center or either end. There's plenty of room for birds at these feeders. The trays measure 12 and 14 inches. Not to worry; they're securely mounted to the window with four large suction cups.

Rose Bernstein of Rockville, Maryland, told us about a house finch that caught his head in the feed hopper of the Twin Hopper feeder. Looker Products is making modifications to eliminate this problem. These feeders are not squirrel proof.

2

FRUIT AND NECTAR FEEDERS

Many birds can be attracted to fruit and nectar feeders. Hummingbirds are the best known, but several larger birds will join them at nectar feeders with perches, including woodpeckers, finches, tanagers, thrushes, warblers, nuthatches, titmice, and orioles. The list of fruit eaters who visit feeders is even longer: mockingbirds, catbirds, robins, starlings, thrushes, waxwings, tanagers, orioles, towhees, bluebirds, yellow-breasted chats, house finches, Carolina wrens, rose-breasted grosbeaks, red-bellied woodpeckers, cardinals, brown thrashers, and jays.

If you want to attract only hummingbirds, first get out the red—plant red flowers. Then, when the flowers are in bloom, try a small feeder with no perches. Hummingbirds will hover at a nectar feeder and, if you provide perches, will sit while feeding. If you live in the West and want to see several species of hummingbirds, try a large nectar feeder with perches.

Nectar feeders come in several styles, made of glass, plastic, or pottery. When deciding on one, first consider how often you're willing to clean it. Glass and pottery are more resistant to the elements than plastic. Next, consider where you'll hang it. Off a window, from a tree limb, or on a pole are the major choices.

If you've ever had a pet gerbil, you're familiar with hanging vacuum water tubes. When they don't drip they're great; when they drip, you have a mess. Fill one of those water tubes with sugar water, and you have a hummingbird feeder.

Whether the feeder is going to be in the sun or the shade is also important. Because hot water expands, you shouldn't fill it to the top or hang the feeder in direct sun. Try a roof overhang near a window or beneath a shaded tree, or hang it in the shade of a hanging basket. Depending on the size of the feeder perch, you could also get larger birds.

Be particularly careful with nectar feeders that attach to a window with suction cups. They may drip on the sill, and when the suction fails, your feeder has nowhere to go but down.

While you're thinking about location, keep in mind that hummingbirds are attracted to anything red: flowers, clothing, lipstick. (While backpacking in the Idaho mountains, Bill saw a hummingbird try to pull nectar from a red sock that was hanging out to dry.) The red on the feeder helps attract the birds, but attaching your feeder to a hanging basket of red fuschia, impatiens, or geraniums is as close as you can get to a guarantee.

It's serendipity with larger birds. Put an oriole nectar feeder near your seed feeders. You don't have to wait until spring to do this, either. And nectar is a treat even in the dead of winter. Sooner or later a curious house finch will give it a try. All it takes is one bird to give a feeder some action. It isn't long before others overcome their reluctance. Likewise, often the mere presence of fruit near seed feeders can excite the birds. You can offer fruit on a tray feeder with spikes, or in a large wire cage.

Check with your local Audubon chapter or bird club for the estimated arrival dates for birds you want to see. In the Northeast, hummers return around the time the azaleas are in bloom. If you want to see orioles, hang up your feeders before the trees leaf out. But if you've missed the spring, don't despair. It's okay to put out fruit and nectar feeders anytime, including winter.

Nectar and Fruit

The nectar formula is simple: measure one-quarter cup granulated sugar into a cup and fill it with boiling water. Some books recommend using honey for its nutritional value, but please don't. Honey can harbor a fungus that hurts hummingbird tongues. And don't offer nectar made with artificial sweeteners. Birds need the extra calories.

Several manufacturers sell liquid nectar fortified with vitamins, minerals, and red food coloring. If you can make your own, you'll save yourself a lot of money. There's no honey in commercial nectar mixes, so they won't harm the birds. But there's no scientific evidence that hummingbirds need or prefer fortified nectar. Wild birds get their protein and nutrients from natural sources. Stick to granulated sugar.

What about red food coloring? Manufacturers put red dye in hummingbird nectar for two reasons: hummingbirds are attracted to red, and the red coloring helps you keep track of how much nectar is left in the feeder. For years people added red coloring to nectar. The myth that red dye is harmful to hummers began years ago, when the alarm went out about Red Dye Number 2, a human carcinogen. The dye currently used in hummingbird food is perfectly safe for *them*.

Do you need red flowers to attract hummingbirds? It helps. Look at the plants hummers visit, and you can't miss the color connection. But there are plenty of flowers other than red-hued ones full of nectar that hummers also visit. A 1971 study of preferences at hummingbird feeders found that the birds will visit feeders of various colors, including those with no color. It may be that hummers learn to seek out red flowers and are willing to poke their tiny bills into other flowers along the way. You don't have to add red coloring. If you do, once hummingbirds have found the feeder, there's no need to continue unless, of course, you want to.

As for offering fruit, as long as it's not rotten, you can't go wrong. Orioles are partial to apples and oranges, cut in half. Mockingbirds, waxwings, and bluebirds like raisins soaked in water. In the summer, tanagers consider bananas, apples, and oranges. Experiment. See which birds you attract with which fruits.

Coping with Insects

Bees, wasps, and ants have wings, too. And they're likely to find whatever fruits and nectar you offer birds. No matter how annoying they might be, don't use insecticides—they kill birds too.

Petroleum jelly instead of salad oil (it can spoil) on your feeder hanger may deter ants. Bee guards—small plastic mesh caps—may keep bees and wasps from getting to the nectar, but they won't keep insects from crowding out your birds. The easiest solution to insect problems is to put out more feeders in different locations. Rest assured; many of the birds you want to attract will eat the insects.

Insecticides are very dangerous to birds *and* humans, despite reassuring advertisements. One of the benefits of attracting birds is that they eat insects.

Rating the Products

Perky Pet Feeders

Perky Pet manufactures the largest and most complete line of nectar feeders and accessories in the industry. Its hummingbird and oriole feeders range in capacity from two to thirty-two ounces.

Our favorite is the Little Beginner tube. It's inexpensive, has just the right capacity (a couple of ounces), and is easy to fill and clean. Just remove the bee guard and run the plastic tube through the dishwasher. The feeder doesn't have perches. You can hang the Little Beginner from your window using an Opus window suction-cup hanger.

We don't recommend the "water bottle with tube"-style, for a couple of reasons: they're difficult to fill and clean, and they're likely to drip.

If you are meticulous about keeping the feeder clean, Perky's no-drip feeders (including one that mounts right on your window) are terrific. But if you don't wash them—with soap—at least once

Hummingbird feeders by Perky Pet

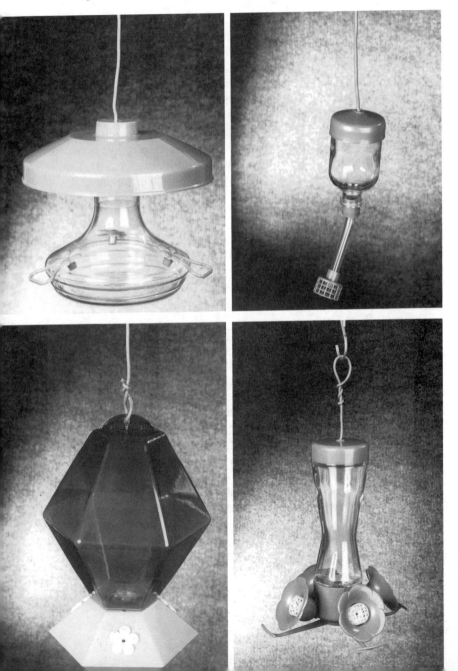

More Perky Pet feeders

a week or more, black mold will grow in the inaccessible feeder base.

You'll need a funnel to fill all but the window feeder. Don't be tempted to fill them to the top. You'll just be wasting nectar. Start out with a small amount, and gradually add more as more birds visit.

Perky has an accessory line that includes a foam cleansing brush and a bracket for mounting the four-flower model to a deck railing or post.

Bruce Barber Feeder Bonnets

Bruce Barber doesn't like the plastic look. His solution? A western red cedar hummingbird feeder bonnet. Your feeder can now look good and stay cool.

Nora Pate Feeders

Nora Pate also had problems with the look of most hummingbird feeders. Her solution was to wrap plain glass test tubes in natural material: eucalyptus bark and bamboo. The results are handsome.

Happy Feeders

Chuck Briggs's Happy Hummingbird and Happy Oriole nectar feeders range in capacity from twelve to thirty-two ounces, and are available with plastic or glass nectar bottles. Most have gaudy white perches and red or orange flower feeding stations with built-in bee guards.

Patlor Hummingbird Survival Kits

Pattie Meade makes vacuum-tube ceramic hummingbird feeders that look like apples, strawberries, cactus, peaches, and oranges. They make great gifts. These feeders hold about a cup of nectar. They come in two styles: plain fruit or with an optional decoration. For example, the apple has a striking purple ceramic hummingbird, and the strawberry has a bumble bee. They work well in the shade.

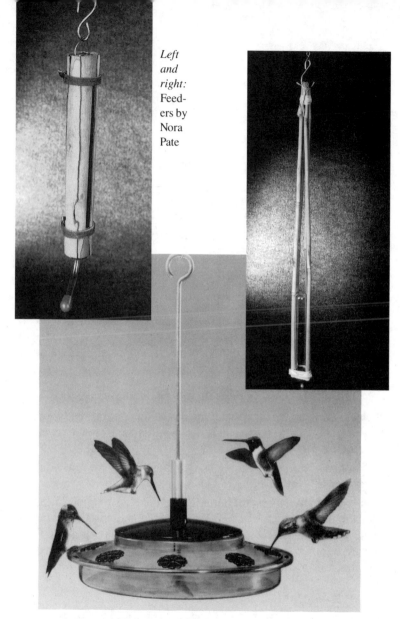

Left and right: Feeders by Nora Pate

The H-8 hummingbird feeder by Droll Yankee

Ceramic Hummingbird Feeders

Any potter can make this one, and you'll see them at just about every craft fair. This one, made by Maryland potter Betsy Wilding, has a large mouth, high-grade tube, and rubber stopper, and is dishwasher safe.

Hummingbird Heaven Hummy Bar and Oriole Fun Bar

Hummingbird Heaven manufactures two glass-tube nectar feeders: the Hummy Bar and the Oriole Fun Bar. They are identical except for the size of the perches and feeding portals, but the oriole feeder is our favorite because it's easy to fill, attractive to small and large birds, and easy to clean.

Droll Yankee LF-1 and H-8

Droll Yankee hummingbird feeders look like flying saucers. Both are made of clear Lexan, with red plastic flower feeding portals sitting on top of the saucers. These no-drip feeders are suspended by a center hanging rod. Three birds can perch on the edge of the small ¾-cup (six-ounce) feeder. Eight birds can visit the quart-size feeder.

If you like the looks of the smaller feeder, be prepared to keep it clean. If mold starts growing inside the feeder portals, there's no way to get inside to clean it. Of the two, the larger feeder is easier to keep clean.

Opus Hummingbird Feeders

Opus manufactures several hummingbird feeders ranging in capacity from eight to forty ounces. We don't recommend their window feeders because they will drip when hot. The Opus egg-shape feeders are another story. They're easy to fill and clean, and have a unique, built-in ant moat to keep ants from getting into the nectar.

Aspects Nectar Bar

The Aspects' window hummingbird feeder uses the same clear plastic shell as their snack bar (4 by 4 by 5 inches). The removable feed-

A ceramic hummingbird feeder by Betsy Wilding

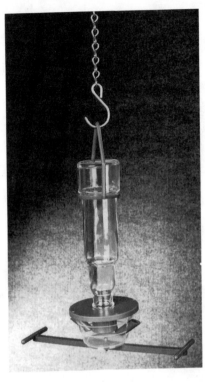

The Hummingbird Heaven Oriole Fun Bar

ing tray has three feeding wells and no perches. The manufacturer says the nectar bar has been carefully designed to thwart bees and other insects. We guess it all depends on your definition of "thwart." Insects have no problem getting into this feeder. It's held to the window by a single suction cup.

Noel's Fruit Wedge

Noel's fruit feeder is a wedge-shape vinyl-dipped metal cage. It measures 9 by 10 by 6 inches and is easy to clean and hang.

Duncraft Fruit Kabob

Duncraft Fruit Kabob is a clear acrylic square with a hole in the center for the skewered fruit to hang. Hang this feeder from the chain and birds are supposed to sit on the perch and enjoy. However, we've never seen a bird use this feeder. The wooden skewer eventually disintegrates, leaving you nothing to put the fruit on.

Oriole Orange Feeder

Put a roof on an 8-inch slab of ¾-inch redwood, red cedar, or stained pine, then add a sharpened dowel to the midsection and a horizontal perch at the base. Cut an orange in half and stab it into the sharpened dowel. You've built an oriole orange feeder. Several companies make this product. They all look the same.

We've never seen an oriole use this feeder, but we've seen pictures. Stained wood looks great, but again, plastic is healthier.

Horizontal Fruit Stake

Nail a small western cedar platform feeder to a tree. Add drainage holes and a lip around the edge, then turn it upside down and put two nails through the bottom, driven up into the platform. Cut an orange in half and stab the halves onto the nails. You've made a fruit stake or, if you put two ears of corn on it, you've made a squirrel feeding platform. Again, plastic is a better material.

Ant Scat and Ant Eliminator

Several companies market ant repellents that hang in a tiny cup at the top of the wire holding your hummingbird feeder. One manufacturer recommends "a few drops of kerosene or diesel fuel" for his copper and brass cup, another comes complete with a supply of wheel bearing grease. Can you believe the lengths manufacturers think people will go to eliminate ants?

Imagine what the heat and wind will do with this tiny cup of poison suspended above your nectar feeder. Better to save your money and put petroleum jelly on the wire. It's inert and won't contaminate your feeder.

3

BAFFLES

Put food out for birds and some creature—bird or otherwise—will find it. Put a nesting box on a tree trunk or limb, and some creature will look upon your invited guests as dinner.

Who are these creatures who interfere with your avian tranquillity? Neighborhood cats, raccoons, opossums, rats, mice, chipmunks, squirrels, snakes, bees and wasps, as well as starlings, house sparrows, kestrels, and sharp-shinned hawks.

What can you do to foil them? That depends. You'll have to tolerate the birds of prey. They're part of the natural system and are protected by federal law. Many birders consider themselves fortunate to witness a hawk or owl at work; it's a breathtaking sight. Without predators, songbird populations would run amok. In addition, these predators weed out the weaker birds, strengthening the species gene pool.

But the other creatures are another story. Mention cats, and people react emotionally. Love them or hate them, both house cats and feral cats take a heavy toll on songbird populations, particularly during nesting season. If you have a feeder or nesting box, you'll soon discover a cat lurking nearby.

You could try reasoning with the cat's owner, but no matter what you say, it's likely to fall on deaf ears. It's not worth arguing with neighbors about the ethics or legality of their unleashed pets. When

cats are present, birds usually are n
Havahart trap or a dog.

Most animal control offices and H
loan traps. You set the trap, catch the c
it to the authorities. But keep in min
increase your popularity in the neig

The most efficient cat control is a
a fenced yard. The same strategy is e
munks, and other daytime unwelcon
a dog, and don't want to add one to yo
and baffles.

If you have a g
don't mind bein
baffle. It will
a little ex
defeat,
feed

Predator guards are supposed to keep unwanted animals from
entering birdhouses and making a dinner of nesting birds. For information on predator guards, see chapter 4, on birdhouses. Baffles
are supposed to keep squirrels, cats, raccoons, and snakes from your
feeders and birdhouses. They should keep unwanted animals from
climbing up the poles and down the hangers, and they are discussed
in the first part of this chapter. The remainder of the chapter dis-
cusses diversionary tactics.

Baffles

Given proper installation, the most effective baffles are pole
mounted. But placement is critical. How high can a squirrel or cat
jump? Try placing the baffle about four feet up the pole, with the
feeder just above it. If you can put your pole at least ten feet from
a squirrel take-off point (from the side or above), a quality baffle
may work. Be prepared to increase the distance as the squirrels defy
death to reach your feeder.

Hanging baffles are less effective. They must be at least ten feet
from a tree trunk, deck rail, fence, or roof.

Squirrels will leap more than ten feet when it's laterally downward. Ruppert Chappell of Rockville, Maryland, actually video-
taped a squirrel running the length of his deck railing to gather the
impetus to vault over *twenty* feet to his feeder.

od sense of humor, need something to do, and
g outwitted by a pint-sized rodent, try a hanging
require constant attention, since squirrels can, with
ra effort, eventually get past them. When you admit
ell yourself you bought the baffle to keep the rain off the
r. It just may do a better job at that.

Your chances of both immediate and sustained success are greater with a pole baffle or a squirrel-proof feeder. We discussed squirrel-proof feeders in chapter 1. But if you are otherwise satisfied with your feeder, then a pole baffle is your next option.

Consider what the baffle is made of. Thus far, steel has proved most effective, followed by—in declining order of effectiveness—sheet metal, aluminum, polycarbonate plastic, and acrylic plastic. The most expensive materials are the most effective.

Baffle design is an obvious factor in its success. Most baffles are domes with holes for the pole to slide through, or domes with hooks from which to hang the feeders. Generally, the larger the diameter, the more effective the baffle. But the stovepipe baffles are the exception. They are effective until squirrels discover they can chew through the aluminum.

Rating the Baffles

Pole Baffles

Droll Yankee Giant Seed Tray/Squirrel Baffle

The Droll Yankee Giant Seed Tray/Squirrel Baffle will fit only the Droll Yankee and the Aspects poles. Made of virtually indestructible Lexan plastic, this baffle is wide enough to stop offending critters, providing you mount it 4 feet up the pole.

Don't use this as a seed tray, unless you drill extra drainage holes. The existing drainage holes are way too small and are easily clogged. Be prepared to clean it often, because it also catches bird droppings.

Gull Lake Baffle

Gull Lake manufactures an attractive black sheet-metal baffle. It's tipsy enough to keep the squirrels slipping off. But all it takes to defeat it is one squirrel pushing the baffle up past the rubber gasket. So far, they're stymied.

Bower Metal Baffle

Bower Company manufactures a metal baffle with a wide diameter. It's held to a pole by a metal spring. As long as the spring stays tight, this baffle does a super job.

The problem is, these baffles don't fit every pole. For example, they don't fit poles by Droll Yankee, Heath, or Gull Lake.

Hyde Stovepipe Metal Baffle

The Hyde Company offers a different metal solution: a 12-inch- and 6-inch-wide aluminum stovepipe baffle with a bracket to fit any post ¾ to 2 inches in diameter. Don Hyde says, "Your money back if it doesn't stop 'em, provided the post, baffle, and feeder are far enough away from buildings and high enough off the ground so a squirrel cannot jump over the baffle." It's not the most visually attractive solution, but we urge you to take Mr. Hyde up on his money-back guarantee.

Heath Baffles

The Heath Company has two attractive clear-plastic baffles: the SB-2 fits ½- to 1¼-inch pole mounts with three set screws, and the SB-3 fits ½- to 1¼-inch pole mounts on a plastic flange with three screws.

Both are made of a plastic squirrels seem to have no trouble chewing through. There's a simple solution: coat the flange and baffle with Vaseline laced with cayenne pepper.

K-Feeder Baffles

The gray polystyrene K-Feeder (KPB) baffle is easy work for squirrels. They just chew through the soft plastic.

Aspects Squirrel Stopper

The Aspects Squirrel Stopper metal baffle has two flaws: the diameter is too small and squirrels can chew through the plastic gasket holding the feeder to the pole. Aspects is working on a new design.

Hanging Baffles

Several companies manufacture plastic domes designed to be hung from a chain or heavy-duty rope. Generally, squirrels don't chew through these baffles. They are content to slide down past them and grab hold of the feeder perch or tray. For best results, don't hang a feeder with perches and a tray from a baffle. If you can, remove them.

In selecting a hanging baffle, remember that wider is better. Polycarbonate, Lexan, and metal are the most effective materials. The small-diameter domes work best to keep starlings from feeding comfortably at suet feeders.

Before you walk out of the store with your baffle, check to see that all the parts (washers, hangers) are in the box.

4

FOOD FOR THE BIRDS

If you've ever been to a New York City delicatessen, you've probably been overwhelmed by the enormous variety of food that's available. "What should I order?" is the common dilemma that most deli visitors confront. Bird enthusiasts have a similar problem: "Which seed should I choose for my backyard birds?" In this chapter we've tried to answer that question by taking a close look at seeds, suet, and bluebird feeders. (We examined fruit and nectar feeders in chapter 2.)

Seed Options

If you put out a birdfeeder and fill it with seed, no matter where you live, wild birds are sure to visit. They may arrive immediately or it may take days, weeks, or months for them to find it. Be patient: eventually they will come. Birds find their food by using visual cues. Often all it takes is one curious creature, and in short time the feeder is full of birds. The key to attracting seed-eating birds is knowing their seed preferences and which feeders work best.

Identify your desired visitors, then learn as much as you can about them. Different species visit backyards for different reasons. If you don't want to spend much money, all you need is a bath to attract most birds. Others will frequent your yard because you also offer food. Still others will stay because they use nesting boxes.

There are many misconceptions regarding birdfeeding. Until very recently, most people set out commercial seed mixes. They based their selection on the belief that the wider the seed variety, the wider the variety of bird species attracted. But mixes are not the best products to feed birds. Watch birds at a mixed-seed feeder as they kick seeds onto the ground. Birds eat a lot like adolescent humans; they pick out what they like.

A study by the U.S. Fish and Wildlife Service found that birds have specific preferences at feeding stations, and that no standard mix satisfies all the birds in your backyard. For best results, the study suggested offering black-oil sunflower seed and white proso millet in separate feeders.

Try it. We're confident you'll save yourself considerable money and aggravation by not using mixes of any kind. Birds have no reason to kick out seeds from feeders full of one kind of seed.

Separate seeds in separate feeders eliminates wasted seeds and mess under the feeder. It also minimizes the likelihood of birds picking up diseases by eating the seeds exposed to bird droppings and other contaminants in the soil under the feeder.

Be sure to store your seed in a cool, dry place (a metal garbage can in your basement, garage, or shaded patio). During the summer, buy just enough seed to fill your feeder, and leave the storage problem to your retailer.

Sunflower Versus Other Seed

Sunflower seeds come in several varieties: black oil, gray-striped, black-striped, hulled (chips or kernels), and Finch Choice (a processed sunflower product).

1. *Black-oil sunflower seed.* The U.S. Fish and Wildlife Service study found this seed to be "superior to other foods for most species. . . . Some of the birds ordinarily regarded as small seed eaters found oil-type sunflower attractive; white-throated sparrows, song sparrows,

black-oil sunflower seed

house sparrows and dark-eyed juncos all made significant use of oil-type sunflower seeds even when white proso millet was available." Studies by the Cornell Laboratory of Ornithology confirmed the U.S. Fish and Wildlife Service study: most birds prefer black-oil over striped sunflower seeds. In taste tests, chickadees showed a two-to-one preference for black-oil, apparently with good reason because the black-oil has a higher seed-to-shell ratio and a higher oil content.

2. *Black-striped sunflower seed.* The U.S. Fish and Wildlife Service study found that "only tufted titmice and blue jays preferred black-striped

sunflower to other sunflower products." Many other birds will consume it.

3. *Gray-striped sunflower seed.* According to the study, "All species that liked sunflower seeds ate the gray-striped seed, but they usually consumed less of the gray-striped than the oil or black-striped."

There are two other forms of sunflower seed on the market: hulled sunflower (also called chips and kernels) and Finch Choice. Finch Choice is a processed hulled sunflower, crushed to fit in a thistle feeder and coated with a corn syrup protein to protect the seed from humidity. Hulled sunflower seeds are striped sunflower seeds without the shell. The U.S. Fish and Wildlife Service study found these seeds to be very attractive to "American goldfinches, house sparrows and white-throated sparrows." Hulled sunflower seeds are the no-mess food. Because there's no shell to protect the kernel from humidity, hulled sunflower seeds tend to cake in feeders, so use them in low-capacity feeders.

Other kinds of seed include:

1. *White proso millet.* The U.S. Fish and Wildlife Service study recommended that millet "be the food of choice in any feeding program to attract dark-eyed juncos, mourning doves, and all species of sparrows. . . . Its relatively low cost and high attractiveness make it an excellent food. . . ."

2. *Red proso millet.* According to the study, this "can be used as a substitute for white proso millet, although it is apparently somewhat less attractive."

3. *Golden millet.* The study found this was "in no instance . . . as attractive as white proso millet, but it was superior to black-striped sunflower in attracting brown-headed cowbirds and house sparrows."

4. *Milo (sorghum).* The study concluded: "Although milo is a common ingredient in wild bird mixes, in view of its general unattractiveness it probably should not be used."

5. *Mixed bird seed.* Many of the ingredients routinely included in wild bird mixes are generally unattractive to the extent that, even with their lower cost, they do not provide the bird visits per unit cost afforded

by white proso millet. Commonly used, essentially unattractive foods are wheat, milo, peanut hearts, hulled oats, and rice.

6. *Cracked corn.* The study pointed out that fine cracked corn "is eaten about one third as often as white proso millet."

7. *Safflower seed.* Safflower seed was not included in the U.S. Fish and Wildlife Service study. What we know about its effectiveness in feeding programs is anecdotal. None of the birds who visit feeders seem to favor it. But cardinals, doves, and house finches will eat it if you do not offer sunflower seed. Most people use safflower seed because squirrels don't seem to like it. Try some in a wooden house feeder, because squirrels may leave a safflower-stuffed feeder alone.

8. *Canary seed.* No birds in the study found this as attractive as white proso millet. "Since it costs about 70% more than white proso millet, little advantage accrues from adding this seed to mixes, and certainly none in presenting it alone."

9. *Rape seed.* According to the study feeders with rape seed "received no visits by any bird. . . . It was the least attractive food in this study."

10. *Wheat seed.* The U.S. Fish and Wildlife Service study found that, "of the species that used wheat, all used black-striped sunflower or white proso to a much greater extent."

11. *Flax seed.* This "was almost completely ignored by all species."

12. *Oats.* The inclusion of hulled oats is ill advised because "the only species finding them strongly attractive was starlings."

13. *Peanut hearts.* They are "extremely attractive to starlings." We recommend them to fortify homemade suet.

14. *Peanut kernels.* These "are remarkably attractive. Tufted titmice, blue jays, Carolina chickadees and white-throated sparrows readily took to this food." Woodpeckers like it, too.

Thistle Seed

Thistle seed in the U.S. Fish and Wildlife Service study "demonstrated excellence as a goldfinch food. It also was eaten to a significant extent by house and purple finches, mourning doves, song sparrows, white-throated sparrows and dark-eyed juncos." Thistle is a black sliver of a seed, a purple-flowered prickery plant that grows along roadsides and fields. Considered a noxious weed, it is an important source of food and nesting material for the American goldfinch.

Niger "thistle" seed that is sold for feeders is not the same plant. It's the most expensive seed on the market today because it's imported from Ethiopia and India, and sterilized at port of entry. If you see thistles sprouting under the feeder, don't worry because the seed won't grow more than an inch or so.

According to the U.S. Fish and Wildlife Service study, thistle is not a first choice for any birds who visit feeders. Finches will eat it, as will an occasional mourning dove and white-throated sparrow, or squirrels when they are exceptionally hungry.

That so few birds are interested in thistle makes it a good alternative seed for attracting finches. Just about all the birds who visit feeders compete with finches for the favorite, hulled sunflower seeds. So if you want to see finches at a feeder, thistle is the best choice. Thistle is also a relatively mess-free food. The shells are so tiny they blow away. It's ideal for decks, apartment balconies, and small yards. Finches will come to window feeders, nylon mesh sacks, and tube feeders.

If you've never used thistle before, be patient. The birds may find it right away, or it might take week or months. Try putting some aluminum foil around the top or bottom of the feeder to attract attention.

When you buy a new feeder, clean it in hot soapy water with a capful of bleach before you put it out. If you've had an active sunflower feeder, consider taking it down for a week and replacing it with the thistle feeder. Birds are creatures of habit. They'll visit the new feeder expecting sunflower. Let them get used to the thistle for a couple of days, then bring your sunflower feeder back out.

If you've had finches visiting your feeder, and all of a sudden they disappear, your feeder is probably due for a cleaning, or your seed is spoiled. Birdseed will spoil if it gets wet, and thistle seems to be particularly susceptible to moisture. Rain and humid summers can quickly ruin seed in both mesh and plastic tube feeders.

If your feeder is clean, your seed is dry, and you still don't see any finches, don't give up. They may just be feasting on natural food supplies. When they're nesting and the weather is lousy, birds look for your feeder. Watch for them at dawn and dusk.

If you live on the East Coast, you may have a problem bird at your thistle feeder—the house finch. Over the past few years this West Coast native has literally taken over sunflower and thistle feeders, bullying smaller birds including goldfinches. You can slow down the house finches at sunflower tube feeders by removing the perches. Likewise, reducing perch size to a half-inch or less on thistle feeders will deter the house finches without affecting the goldfinches.

Grit

In the winter you may notice flocks of birds along the roadsides after the snowplows have passed. The birds are after the sand. Birds have no teeth to grind their food. The dirt, sand, pebbles, and grit they eat sits in their crop and helps break up the food.

Adding grit to your feeder is helpful year-round, but particularly in the winter and spring. Crushed eggshells do the same thing, and in the spring have an added benefit of providing extra calcium for egg formation during nesting season.

Feeding Strategies

Because seed-eating birds have distinct feeding preferences, the best advice we can offer is to use separate seeds in separate feeders: thistle or Finch Choice for finches; sunflower seed for woodpeckers, cardinals, chickadees, nuthatches, finches, mourning doves, and grosbeaks; safflower seed for cardinals, finches, and doves; millet for doves and sparrows; fine cracked corn for ducks, geese, and quail; and peanut kernels for titmice, woodpeckers, and jays.

For years, seed manufacturers have sold seed mixes containing a white millet base with sunflower and some colorful seeds like red millet and milo added. The key word here is "colorful"—seeds that look good in the feeder. Regardless of manufacturer, and some are better than others, mixed birdseed is not a good buy.

It seems that the proliferation of specialized birdseed, gourmet birdseed, hulled birdseed, nutritiously designed birdseed, and scientifically blended birdseed has had one result: birds can now choose the seed they want. If you put out supermarket birdseed in your yard, the birds may just snub your house for the house across the street with the shelled peanuts and sunflower seed from Pennsylvania. Of course, this phenomenon hasn't occurred yet, but as birdfeeding grows more and more popular, and as birdseed becomes more exotic, who knows? Here's our evaluation of common seed mixes.

Rating the Seed Mixes

Purina Songberry Mix

Purina created a unique product called Songberry. Here cereal grains and sunflower are joined with colorful processed berry bits made with real fruit and natural berry flavors. Rodents love it. Birds don't seem to notice the berries; they're too interested in the sunflower.

Seaboard National Audubon Society Premium Mix

The National Audubon Society has sold Seaboard, a Chicago-based seed company, an exclusive license to manufacture and distribute products called National Audubon Society Premium Wild Bird Food. This is the only wild bird food formulated and endorsed by the National Audubon Society.

Available in bags or a handy reusable plastic pail, the label lists the ingredients: sunflower, millet, and peanuts. From the way it's listed, you might expect to see a blend rich with sunflower, less millet, and a few peanuts. You may be wrong. Our bucket of seed contains a lot of millet, a handful of sunflower seed, and nary a peanut. Unlike human food, the order of ingredients on the label does not always correspond to the quantity. We also found milo, not listed on the label. What's wrong with that? This is a premium brand; it costs more. You should be getting more sunflower and less millet. It's just another example of how manufacturers play on consumers' expectations of endorsements. We're amazed that, after the results of the U.S. Fish and Wildlife Service study, the National Audubon Society continues to endorse mixed bird seed products.

Kaytee Birdseed Mixes

You're likely to see Kaytee wild bird seed on your supermarket shelves. The Chilton, Wisconsin, company manufactures one of the best wild bird mixes on the market, and its packaging is honest and full of accurate information about birdfeeding. Kaytee offers three mixes: songbird food, wild bird food, and wild finch food.

If you're determined to use a mix, Kaytee's is the best: black-oil sunflower, striped sunflower, cracked corn, millet, peanuts, and sunflower hearts (in that order of abundance). Kaytee's wild bird food and wild finch mixes are less effective. The wild bird food is millet, milo, wheat, corn, and sunflower fortified with vitamins and minerals. The finch food is a mix of canary seed, niger thistle, rape, finch millet, white millet, red millet, flax, and calcium.

Lyric Birdseed Mixes

Lyric, a Stanford Seed Company, also manufactures several mixes, distinguished by the percentage of sunflower seeds.

The Supreme mix is 40 percent sunflower (black-striped, black oil, and gray-striped), with white millet, safflower, fine cracked corn, niger, peanut hearts, golden millet, canary, and hemp. Quack 'N Snack is a mix, Lyric says, for ducks, geese, deer, quail, wild turkeys, pheasants, chipmunks, and squirrels. It contains whole yellow corn, wheat, oats, milo, proso millet, roasted shelled peanuts, sunflower, kibbled corn, canary seed, green peanuts in the shell, flaked corn, sweet rape, and buckwheat.

Extra is 20 percent sunflower (striped and black oil), white millet, cracked corn, safflower, niger, peanut hearts, golden millet, hemp, and canary seed. Value is 10 percent sunflower (black-oil and striped), white millet, fine cracked corn, and safflower. Finch

Mix is sunflower "bits and pieces," niger, canary, sesame, and golden millet.

If you select Finch Mix, you can be assured of attracting a variety of colorful birds including finches, goldfinches, titmice, doves, cardinals, nuthatches. The seed is designed not to appeal to a particular species—though finches like it the best—but to bring a number of species to your yard.

Bay-Mor Mixes

Bay-Mor manufactures four bird mixes and one squirrel mix. The Bay-Mor premium mix, Rhapsody, is 30 percent black-oil sunflower seed with white millet, peanut hearts, wheat, and milo.

Sonne Labs Finch Choice

The problem, of course, with trying Finch Choice is that if it works, there are going to be a whole lot of finches in the yard. Lots of birds like the stuff. This includes beautiful goldfinches, but unfortunately also sparrows and house finches. On the plus side, titmice and nuthatches will also dine on Finch Choice. Every birdlover has his or her preference when it comes to desirable backyard birds; we rank goldfinches above house finches above sparrows. Of course, many people want to attract a multitude of birds, as well as a variety.

Finch Choice is a "nouveau" birdseed. It's gourmet food. If birds could read the label, they'd think they were getting a really great meal. The product boasts its ingredients:

> Sunflower, soybean oil, corn protein and color [black and gray]. Analysis: Crude Protein (min 20%), Crude Fat (min 20%), Crude Fiber (max 8%), Moisture (max 10%), Ash (max 5%).

Color? Who's crazy enough to put coloring into bird seed? Well, when you stop to think about it, color isn't necessarily a bad thing—in fact, food color in birdseed has practical benefits. Just as you wouldn't expect birds to go for turquoise-colored seed, you might anticipate that goldfinches and other thistle-loving birds would have their eyes out for food that's the same color as thistle seed—and you get it at a fraction of the price. From a distance, black-colored seed looks a lot tastier than many other colors.

Because birds can also mistake Finch Choice for sunflower seed, cardinals and other sunflower-seed lovers will munch on it. Alas, so will squirrels.

Is food coloring bad for birds? The answer is yes and no. Food coloring probably is bad for birds, but birds don't live long enough for coloring to have an adverse effect on their lives.

Suet

If you're looking to offer a menu with variety, consider adding a suet feeder. Woodpeckers, chickadees, titmice, wrens, creepers, and nuthatches love suet the way some people love chocolate cake. (Suet is much more nutritious for birds, however.) Bluebirds, cardinals, finches, and sparrows will give it a try as well. Before you panic at the thought of woodpeckers in your backyard, let's clear up some of the myths about them.

- Woodpeckers do not kill trees.
- Woodpeckers will not destroy your house.

The appearance of woodpeckers, other than at your feeder, is often the first warning of the presence of their favorite meal: wood-boring insects like termites, carpenter bees, and carpenter ants. If birds are pecking away at your backyard pine, it's often because the tree harbors a woodpecker delicacy. Woodpeckers usually choose dying or dead trees with soft rotted insides for their nesting sites. If they're pecking at your cedar or redwood siding, it's likely your house is infested. Don't blame the woodpeckers for the dime-size holes in your cedar siding. That's the work of carpenter bees.

Suet may cut down on woodpecker pecking of your house by giving them an alternative source of food. (Some woodpecker pecking is related to mating behavior, some has to do with eating.) So if you have woodpecker problems, there may be no better reason to put up a suet feeder.

One member of the woodpecker family suffers particularly bad press. The name "sapsucker" may send chills up the spine of treelovers. But there's really nothing to fear. These small birds leave a circle of tiny scars on your trees, but they're not likely to kill them.

Sapsuckers eat the soft inner bark and sap of over two hundred native trees, including birches, aspens, and apples. They also eat fruits and berries. They get their protein from leaf-eating insects, ants, wasps, and flies.

We'd like to say woodpeckers won't visit your house if there's no insect problem. But there's more to the story. In the spring, male woodpeckers may use your house as a drum. Almost like teenagers, during breeding season woodpeckers are out to make a lot of noise. Before aluminum siding and gutters, the birds used the natural resonance of trees to signal their territorial boundaries and to attract females. But an occasional clever woodpecker has discovered that some houses have more resonance. That's all very interesting until he chooses your house.

If you've ever been awakened before dawn by a crow-size woodpecker drumming away at the tree next to your bedroom window, or worse, your windowsill, your first thought is not likely to be "Gee, isn't that great, a pileated woodpecker—the largest woodpecker in North America—right at my window." If it happens to you, ignore your first impulse. These spectacular creatures are protected by federal and state laws. If the woodpecker persists, try scare devices such as balloons, metal pie pans, and reflective tape. If all fails, cover the area with plastic bird netting.

What Is Suet?

Suet, otherwise known as animal fat, is probably the closest thing to fast-food for birds. It's high in calories and easy to digest.

Which fat is preferred? Some authors recommend vegetable shortening. Others suggest rendering bacon drippings and kitchen scraps.

Unlike the U.S. Fish and Wildlife Service's study on seed preferences, there's little or no scientific data on suet preferences and nutritional value. However, it's safe to say that beef fat is readily eaten, simply because bird-food manufacturers have used it for years. Beef fat is easy to obtain and easy to handle. Ask a butcher for suet, and you're likely to get beef kidney fat. That's because huge quantities of fat cushion the kidneys. But sometimes you'll get strips of fat trimmed from other cuts. It's all the same. Fat is fat, regardless of its anatomical origin.

When the weather's cold, just put strips or chunks of fat in a suet holder. You don't have to worry about the fat spoiling. You'll know it's gone bad when it sports a black malodorous crust.

Birds appreciate the extra calories during cold weather. They'll also frequent suet feeders when they need the extra calories during migration and breeding season. Keep your feeder full year-round, and you may witness pair-bonding behavior and frustrated parents harassed by fledglings. As the weather gets warmer, raw beef fat is likely to cause problems: it may drip and become rancid. Is it safe to offer suet in the summer?

Again, it's hard to say since there have been no scientific studies. If you offer suet in warm weather, consider using rendered suet. Rendering, or boiling, kills bacteria and removes moisture, thus prolonging the life of your suet. Rather than adding mixed bird seed, consider peanut hearts or moist dog food (both better sources of protein). These ingredients seem to bind the fat, minimizing dripping and crumbling.

If you like to cook, rendering suet may be fun the first time you try it. When it gets tedious (and smelly), consider the convenient commercial suet cakes. There is a down side to offering suet, though. It's messy for humans. We defy you to fill most suet feeders without getting your hands greasy.

Rating the Suet Products

Suet Cakes and Cake-Holder Combinations

There are four basic suet formulas: plain, insect, peanut, and seed cakes. Since there are no scientific data available, we recommend you try each and decide for yourself. Aside from price, make your decision based on your answers to these questions:

- Does it attract the birds you want?
- Does it attract animals you don't want?
- How readily does it melt?

Maine Manna, C & S Suet, Heath, Bishop, Nelson Products, Lyric, and several other companies manufacture suet cakes fortified with seed mixtures, usually a blend of sunflower seed, corn, millet, milo, safflower, and peanuts. Remember, birds have seed preferences, and given a choice, they pick their favorites and toss away the rest. A considerable amount of these cakes end up on the ground under the feeder.

C & S Plain Suet

It's not easy to find rendered plain suet. We were amazed to find that it often costs more than peanut or seed suet. C & S Products' plain beef suet comes in a plastic tub and fits in a round suet barrel. Remove the plastic top, pop it into the barrel top down, and you've got the no-mess solution.

Starlings and squirrels tend to leave this additive-free suet alone. But it's one of the first to drip in warm weather.

Cockerum Oregon Insect Suet

Operating on the premise that birds who visit suet benefit more from insect protein than seed, Cockerum Oregon Insects created three suet-insect products: Oregon Suet Cake, Suet Block, and Suet Cone.

These pricey products are 99 percent rendered beef kidney suet and 1 percent crushed, dehydrated housefly larvae, pupae, and adults. Contrary to the manufacturer's promise, our Oregon Suet Block was quick to melt in warm weather. But what may well be the major advantage of this product is that starlings don't seem to like it.

COI has introduced another new suet-insect product: Blue Robin Crumbles for bluebirds. It's a modified version of miracle meal, the bluebird food promoted in the North American Bluebird Society's Newsletter "Sialia."

Cockerum Oregon Insect Suet Block

BLUE ROBIN CRUMBLES
Suet
Cornmeal
Housefly parts
Whole-wheat flour

MIRACLE MEAL
1 cup flour
3 cups yellow cornmeal
Add spoonfuls of lard (not vegetable shortening) until firm
Peanut butter (optional)

In the wild, bluebirds are attracted to fruits and berries. Should you have the good fortune to have bluebirds in your yard, consider growing one of their favorite food plants, *fosteri* holly. Bluebirds will also consider raisins and peanut chips in a special bluebird feeder.

Peanut Suet

If you want to attract birds who eat peanuts, peanut suet is your best bet, and almost every birdseed company manufactures peanut suet. Peanut suet will quickly be a favorite of chickadees, Carolina wrens, titmice, and downy woodpeckers. We've seen cardinals hover like hummingbirds under a feeder full of peanut suet.

Fat Stuff

Unfortunately, starlings and squirrels go for the peanuts, too. Hang it in a starling-resistant feeder on a squirrel-proof pole. Or use Noel's Restrictive Wire Feeder with the metal top.

Fat Stuff

All right, we wouldn't buy something to eat called Fat Stuff. And it's not the kind of food that even a fast-food restaurant's likely to admit serving. But do the birds like this brand of suet? We gave Fat Stuff to our evaluation center.

Fat Stuff ordinary suet comes inside a screwlike coil that gives birds a place on which to perch while they eat. Fat Stuff is wrapped in cellophane. The coil holds it so tightly that you can't push or pull it out. And you can't remove the wrapping while it's in the coil. Instead, you have to turn the coil while holding the suet in place. Or just leave it in the wrapping. The birds will peck away at it.

Once you have the suet out, reinsert the metal rod through the suet and screw on the eye washer. This is the classic definition of messy. Fat Stuff is a completely self-contained suet feeder, with a hook on top, so you don't need a suet basket. When it's empty, you dispose of the whole contraption. Birds like it.

Suet Bells

Suet bells are suet in a convenient disposable plastic mesh bag dispenser. Birds fly to the bell and hang on to the mesh bag while they're eating. One of the biggest problems with this type of feeder is that it's messy in warm weather—messy for you and messy for the birds. They have to hang on to the thin, greasy mesh bag. If the suet drips, it gets on their feathers.

There has been one report of a downy woodpecker at a suet feeder in warm weather who developed a feather follicle infection, causing him to lose facial feathers. There's no proof that the suet caused the infection, but it makes sense to avoid suet dripping on bird feathers. Maine Manna makes mixed seed suet bells. Lyric makes peanut butter bells.

Suet 'N Seed

Suet 'N Seed is a good, all-purpose suet. It provides ample fat to birds in the winter and attracts woodpeckers all year round. Like most commercial suets, Suet 'N Seed can be used in the summer. It comes in several different sizes, and the larger suet cakes are available with their own suet baskets. Because a suet container is a rather messy thing to refill, the large sizes are nice. One warning, however: if squirrels frequent your yard, they will probably eat through the suet net, causing the suet to fall to the ground.

Basic Suet Feeders
Suet Sacks

These are reusable nylon and vinyl net bags to hold suet. The ¾-inch mesh, heavy-duty cloth bags from Dartmouth last longer and offer thicker perches than many suet bags offered by other manufacturers. Clean them regularly in hot soapy water.

Suet Cages

Metal suet cages provide a stable place for birds to perch. Galvanized rustproof metal is preferred; don't use chicken wire or other thin, sharp wire. It's likely to cut the birds' feet, making them susceptible to disease. Consider larger mesh sizes if you want to attract the pileated woodpecker.

Should you be concerned if the metal cage is not plastic coated? No. Birds' feet will not freeze to metal perches. The same goes for their eyes—they won't freeze to metal either. No healthy bird would touch his eye to metal while feeding.

If there's a problem with metal suet cages, it's size. Cages come in all sizes and shapes. If you use commercial cakes, find the feeder that fits the cake. Some, particularly the one-cake feeders from Hyde Company and Ketchum, are just a tad too small for standard suet cakes. If you don't want to get suet all over your hands, use half a cake in these feeders. Or better yet, shop around. Cages from Noel's, Dartmouth, and C & S Products are a perfect fit.

Suet Holders

Dave Eastman, of Country Ecology, makes a suet log from a 12-inch piece of New England white birch. He routs out 1-inch holes and adds wooden dowel perches. Your job is to cram suet into the holes. Why birch? Because birch is a soft wood many birds are attracted to naturally, since the tree is susceptible to insect infestations. But before you buy this feeder, ask yourself—how are you going to clean it?

Vari-Crafts manufactures an attractive suet hut made of a white PVC tube with a red cedar roof. You'll get your hands greasy filling this one, but the birds won't get greasy getting it out. Use only rendered cakes with this feeder.

Starling- and Squirrel-Resistant Suet Feeders

Unfortunately, suet feeders attract creatures other than woodpeckers, wrens, and chickadees. You may have to protect your feeder

Dartmouth suet sack and suet cage

The Dave Eastman
Suet Log

from the occasional dog or raccoon. For these, experiment with height and baffles.

Starlings are another story. A sharply curved dome baffle may be all you need to protect your suet from starlings, since they do not like to hang upside down to feed. Your starlings may adapt to hanging upside down; ours have not—yet. Another inexpensive solution is to nail your suet cage under a 12-inch round piece of scrap wood or metal.

If looks are important, consider the starling-resistant suet feeders made by the Arthur C. Brown Company and Cedarline. Arthur C. Brown's suet feeder is a western red cedar box with a wire mesh bottom. Cedarline's is the same style but made of gray-stained white cedar with a rope hanger instead of a chain.

The Arthur C. Brown Suet Feeder   Noel's starling-resistant suet feeder

Noel's Birdfeeders manufactures a sturdy plastic (easier to clean) starling-resistant suet feeder. The suet (a small Maine Manna bell fits perfectly) sits in a small cage suspended from a 12-inch round yellow plastic roof, surrounded top and bottom by sturdy plastic-coated wire mesh. Small birds dart in and out through the wire mesh. Large birds hang from underneath.

If you can keep these feeders away from squirrels, all three will deter starlings. Their only vulnerability is the roof. Squirrels will chew right through them to get to the suet. The solution? A metal suet feeder. Noel's has manufactured a metal cap for its feeders.

C & S Products offers a unique solution: Take one of their twenty-eight-ounce plastic suet tubs, soak it in hot water or micro-wave it for a minute on high (to loosen the suet from the sides of the plastic tub), remove the plastic top, and put the suet tub upside down in a round suet basket.

Squirrels have a hard time getting their teeth to the suet. Granted, they can get some suet from the bottom, but it's almost too much of an effort. The other nice thing about the tub suet is that you don't get your hands dirty putting the greasy food into the cage.

If you hang the suet near your window, use a bracket. If the suet is too close to the window, you're likely to find that the window turns from clear to something less desirable.

A wooden suet feeder by Heath Company

If you don't like the looks of metal, the Heath Company has a wooden suet feeder that accommodates both square and tub suet cakes. Wooden suet feeders are more difficult to keep clean, because wood is absorbent and can harbor bacteria.

Bluebird Feeders

Keeping other birds from getting to bluebird food is the major problem you'll face when you want to feed bluebirds. There are three basic bluebird feeder styles: the house feeder, the plastic hopper feeder, and the suet log.

Bruce Barber's Plastic Hopper Feeder is by far the best made— ¾-inch western cedar with brass screws. At first glance, it looks just like a sunflower seed house feeder, but there's a 1½-inch hole about 6 inches high on the wooden side, and there's no room for seed to fall past the plastic hopper. You open the top, drop in some Miracle Meal, peanut chips, and raisins. The bluebirds hop through the hole, grab the food, and hop back out.

The Arthur C. Brown Company's ¾-inch western red cedar bluebird unit is a house in the spring; drop down the front panel, and it's a feeder in the winter.

5

GIVING THE BIRDS A DRINK

If your goal is to attract a large variety of birds, a constant supply of open water is critical to your success. If you want to be entertained, bird behavior at a bath beats almost anything you'll see at a feeder or outside a nesting box. Whatever your motivation, providing water is the single most important thing you can do for wild birds. They need it year-round, for drinking and bathing.

Drinking water is particularly important because birds have no salivary glands. Without a nearby source of water, digesting the dry seeds and peanut butter offered at feeding stations can be a formidable task. During most of the year, finding open water isn't much of a problem, but that doesn't mean they won't appreciate your birdbath all the time.

Winter is when birds really need your help finding water. During the cold months, when lakes and rivers are coated with an impenetrable barrier of ice, backyard birdbaths may be their only source of water. You'll get a better idea of how important water is during severe weather when you see flocks of birds eating snow. It's not at all uncommon to see titmice and chickadees hanging tenuously on a sliver of ice, drinking from the tip as it melts in the winter sun.

A bath or water trough has little value if the water in it is frozen. Unfortunately, there's nothing short of adding a heater (more accurately, a warmer) to keep the water from freezing.

In addition to keeping the water open, heaters also protect your bath from water expanding and contracting during the freezing months. Indeed, the biggest problem with leaving baths outside in winter is breakage. Unfortunately, there is no way to prevent ceramic and concrete baths from breaking up after a number of heating and thawing cycles. Commercial sealers help preserve concrete, but a water warmer is the only guaranteed way to add years to the life of your bath.

Birds go about their bathing ritual in a way peculiar to their species. Some birds bathe more often than others. It's not surprising that birds bathe more often in warm weather. For example, chickadees have been known to bathe up to five times a day in summer. While birds don't need to bathe quite as often in winter, bathing is just as important.

Selecting a Location

Unless you're putting out a birdbath for purely altruistic reasons, you can't enjoy it if you can't see it. So pick a spot where it's convenient for your viewing.

Birds are vulnerable when they're wet. They're more likely to take a bath if they can see approaching predators. If you're worried about neighborhood cats, put the bath in the open, on the ground or on a pedestal (the birds don't seem to have a preference), but certainly away from shrubs and other places where predators can hide. Planting a thorny bush in the vicinity (but not too close) or creating a brush pile may make the birds feel more secure.

While it may be tempting, don't put your bath near your feeders. Birds are messy eaters. A bath near a feeder fills up with seeds, shells, and droppings. which contaminate the water in a very short time.

Selecting a Birdbath

How you choose to provide water depends entirely on your sense of esthetics and your pocketbook. The simplest is to put a shallow, gently sloping plastic, ceramic, or metal dish on the ground. A plastic or terra-cotta plant dish or inverted trash-can top will do.

Commercial birdbaths may better suit your landscape plans. The most durable and more expensive baths are made of metal. Poured concrete baths are next, followed in durability by plastic and ceramic.

Birds are most comfortable in a rough-surfaced bath about two feet wide and no more than two inches deep. They're reluctant to use deep baths with steep edges (45 to 90 degrees). If you have a steep, slippery bath, put a large, flat stone or several small ones in the center. This will provide even the smallest bird with a more attractive place to drink or get wet.

Be Patient: The Birds Will Come

One of the first complaints about birdbaths usually comes a couple of days after installation. Not a bird to be seen. But that's not unusual. It may take some time for them to recognize your bath as a source of water. You can hurry recognition by putting your hose in the bath and setting the faucet to a very slow drip. In the wild, birds are attracted more by the sound and movement of water than the sight of still water.

If you don't want to dedicate an outside hose as a birdbath wave and noisemaker, there are alternatives: a leaky bottle or drip and mist faucet attachments.

For the make-it-yourself leaky bottle, any thoroughly cleaned plastic bottle with a handle will do. Fill the container with water and screw the cap on. Hang it by a string from a tree or pole over the bath. Carefully poke a few small holes in the bottom of the bottle to create a slow drip. It should take about a day for the bottle to empty.

If you don't like the looks of this Rube Goldberg noisemaker, purchase a special faucet attachment for your bath. An enterprising Maine entrepreneur has created two attractive products that make water noise: the Mister and the Dripper. Both attach directly to the faucet with a Y flange so you can use your garden hose at the same time.

For more money and effort, you can install a fountain or a pond with a recycling water pump. By far the most attractive and expensive backyard water source is a pond with a waterfall. Tetra and Lotus companies sell kits to make your own waterworks. They range in size from a small fiberglass pool set in a four-foot-square and one-foot-deep wooden box, to full-size koi ponds connected by waterways.

Keep the Bath Clean

No matter what water product you use, your biggest problem is keeping the system clean. Birdbaths, fountains, and shallow ponds are quickly spoiled by the birds (droppings and bathing residues), algae, pollen, and tree debris. Dirty baths may not look very attractive to people, but birds aren't too bright and will use them anyway, often picking up salmonella and other unhealthy things.

For the birds' sake, keep your birdbath clean. Unfortunately, there's no secret product to make cleaning easy. Hose your bath at least once a week (preferably more often), and scrub it with a plastic brush. A capful of bleach in a bucket of dishwashing soap (not detergent) helps with cleaning and sanitation. However, do not mix bleach with any product containing ammonia. Ponds are virtually maintenance-free once the right balance of fish and aquatic plants is achieved.

Rating the Products

Plastic Birdbaths

Plastic birdbaths are lightweight and inexpensive. With minimal maintenance, sturdy polypropylene baths should last several years. They're mar resistant, easy to clean, and resist breaking in very hot and very cold weather.

Plastic is sensitive to ultraviolet radiation. For durability, shade your bath from the sun. Although freezing water will not break plastic baths, an immersible heater is recommended.

Duraco Garden Scene Bath

Duraco manufactures hollow pedestal Garden Scene plastic baths. Installation is simple. Just pick a location, turn the pedestal over, fill it with sand or dirt, plug it and snap the bowl in place.

Plastic baths used to come in only one color, white. Now a more attractive stone-gray is available, as are the decorative yard-furniture colors: Williamsburg blue, beige, steel-gray, rose, and raspberry.

Garden Scene baths stand two feet high. The 19-inch round basin is 2 inches deep with a low center island. Smaller birds are likely to drink from the edge of the bath, and bathe on the island. The plastic surface is easy to clean and sterilize with bleach.

Each bath comes with installation instructions taped to the pedestal cap. Be careful how you install the cap. If you put it on backward, you'll damage the plugs that hold the cap on.

Droll Yankee Water Dish

Droll Yankee manufactures a blue plastic water dish for its pole-mounted birdfeeder system. The instructions suggest that by adding a seed tray or feeder to the pole, you have the convenience of feeding and bathing in one place. Don't. It's almost impossible for one not to contaminate the other.

The 13-inch round water dish is shallow enough, but the edge is steep (90 degrees) and slippery. The best way to use this product is on a pole by itself or with a cover, should you wish to exclude larger birds.

The dish comes with a three-year unconditional guarantee.

Metal Birdbaths

Metal baths are the most durable. They won't break when water freezes in them. They're easy to clean. Cast-bronze baths with sloping sides are expensive works of art. The less expensive steel pans have steep, slippery sides. If you nick the surface plating or paint on the steel pans, they will rust.

Bird Oasis

Dave Arvidson of Iron Design manufactures deck and freestanding metal frames for a shallow, lift-out polypropylene dish bath. Each of the four models has a steel frame finished with a durable forest green enamel paint.

The 14-inch diameter Deck Oasis brings birds to a railing, post, fence, or tree. The bath attaches with two screws to any pre-leveled wooden post.

The three-legged, 17-inch diameter Ground Oasis sits 6 inches above the ground and and holds 5 quarts of water.

Put the Ground Oasis on a 29-inch stand and you've got the Lawn Oasis. It's easy to level: just press any or all of the three legs into the ground.

Stick the Garden Oasis in your flower or rock garden. The four-piece unit includes a ground socket, stem, metal ring, and dish.

Looker Birdbaths

Looker Products manufactures blue steel pans set in red cedar cases that can be mounted on a post or bracket or placed on any level surface.

The 10 by 12 by 2-inch blue enamel, aluminum-plated steel baths are steep (90 degrees) and slippery. Unfortunately, some of the pans did not hold the paint. At this writing, Looker was experimenting with a plastic pan. Regardless of pan material, if you want to see small birds bathe, you will have to add rocks.

The shaded bath comes with a western cedar stand and wooden shade. The shade will keep water about 10 degrees cooler in the summer and cut down on evaporation. Looker recommends putting a B-9 birdbath heater under the pan to keep the water open in the winter.

White Swan Birdbath

White Swan has taken copper, tin, lead, and zinc and melted them to create a 12-inch solid bronze birdbath. There are six models weighing about six pounds each. Just 1½-inches deep, they're just the right angle and depth for most birds, and easiest of all the baths to keep clean. Each is individually cast and hand finished, so they're not inexpensive.

If you're looking for a sundial and a birdbath, take a look at White Swan's; it's absolutely beautiful.

Poured-Concrete and Stone Baths

Poured-concrete baths are a good buy because of what they offer the birds—a rough surface, usually a wide diameter, gentle slopes, and stability—and because of what they offer people—resistance to weathering and good looks.

Concrete baths are simple to make. All you need is one of over a hundred molds and the right mix of sand, Portland gray cement (silica, aluminum, and iron oxide), and clean water. Crushed limestone or marble add to the value of the bath, but are optional.

The retail price of a concrete bath is determined by the cost of the raw ingredients and transportation. If the baths are not made locally, you will pay a tremendous price for shipping.

Concrete is very strong. It can carry the weight of several gallons of water. Thus concrete baths can have wider, deeper basins. But although more weather resistant than plastic baths, non-reinforced concrete is stressed by water as it expands in freezing, and can crack. A coating of sealer will add years to your bath. It's also great for repairing cracks.

What about painted concrete? Suppose you don't like the natural gray. There are two ways to get the colors you want: find a mason willing to pour a bath of more expensive sands (white or black), or paint the bath yourself. To paint the bath, first treat it with a sealer, then paint with swimming-pool paint, epoxy, or chemical-moisture resistant enamels. When properly applied, these paints are not toxic and can extend the life of your bath.

Kamcast Gibraltar Birdbath

The Gibraltar is one of the few birdbaths designed to resemble the place a bird might actually drink. As a result, it easily attracts birds. It's one of the most attractive little birdbaths on the market—a fresh alternative to terra-cotta baths.

Kamcast has created a unique bath designed to sit well in any garden. Five inches high, 20 inches long, and 10 inches wide, the gray or pink marble-colored concrete bath has a terraced depth, alluring to any bird size. The Kamcast bath belongs on the ground surrounded by sand, rocks, or short plants. As far as the birds are

The Kamcast Gibraltar Birdbath

concerned, this is the perfect puddle.

It is not suitable for winter use, since it is too small to hold a heater.

Carruth Studio Kitty and Rabbit Baths

Stone carver George Carruth says about his baths, "My desire is to put a smile in your garden by creating pieces that meld with nature. The images are intended to provide a sense of whimsy or satire." You will smile when you see his cat and rabbit baths. They can be mounted on a concrete pedestal or placed on the ground at the corner of a deck or patio.

The cat is a better buy, if you can live with the irony. Small birds will readily accept its sloping sides. The rabbit is more deeply sloped, therefore more attractive to birds with longer legs. Both are the size of small puddles, perfect for one bird at a time.

Each of Carruth's baths is cast in high-quality fine sand concrete, which acquires its own patina in a relatively short time. They will not survive severe weather and are too small for a heater.

These baths come with complete instructions, but no warranty.

Henfeathers Birdbaths

Instead of concrete, Henfeathers & Company uses bonded marble. The strength of this resin marble makes the baths nearly as durable as lead and bronze, but they weigh and cost much less.

Henfeathers offers two designs: a scallop ground bath with optional cherub and a leaf on a pedestal. The leaf with its shallow and irregular depth is just right for large and small birds. The scallop is deeper, but it can be made more attractive to smaller birds by adding a rock.

Pottery Baths

Pottery baths are an attractive alternative to the heavy concrete birdbaths. They come in all sizes and colors. Some are designed to hang from chains and wires; others mount on metal, wood, or pottery bases. If you have limited space, hanging baths are appealing. Keep in mind that if it hangs, water will spill easily and often.

Pottery baths are porous and will crack if not heated in the winter. Those with glazed surfaces are easy to clean, but some birds may find them too slippery.

Bennington Pottery Bath

Bennington Pottery sells an attractive, shallow terra-cotta bath that can be mounted on a 3-foot wooden stand with steel pegs or hung from aluminum arms. Be careful inserting the steel pegs and aluminum arms. The terra-cotta tends to chip at the insertion holes.

Small birds flock to this bath. But plan to bring the bath in for the winter. It is too shallow for a heater.

Opus Birdbaths

Opus makes two styles of ceramic baths: a 14½-inch round, steep-sloped blue glazed terra-cotta bath that can be hung from a metal chain or placed on a 28-inch black metal stand; and a ground-level gently sloping 24 by 20 by 6-inch ceramic rock bath.

The lightweight ceramic rock is one of the most attractive baths designed for garden placement. While it's likely to be as slippery as the glazed bath, it makes a perfect large puddle. It will not survive the winter and will not take a heater.

The blue bath on a stand can survive the winter with a Nelson Blue Devil birdbath heater.

Top Left:
The Carruth Studio Kitty Bath

Above, left and right: The
Bennington Pottery Terra-Cotta Bath

Below and right: The Opus
Blue Glazed Terra-Cotta Bath

Birdbath Heaters and Heated Baths

Most people put their baths in the garage when the weather gets cold. A heater is too much trouble. After all, how do you get electricity all the way out to your bath?

You need a dedicated outdoor electrical receptacle with a GFCI (ground fault circuit interrupt). Then you need a heater to put in the water.

Your major concern when selecting a heater for outdoor use is safety. Water conducts electricity. A wet heater cord or extension can deliver a deadly jolt. The independent Underwriters Laboratory (UL) tests electrical appliances to determine whether they comply with recognized standards. Products that advertise a UL 499 listing have been evaluated for temperature, enclosure, strength, and cold impact. Several manufacturers of heaters advertise that parts (plug, cord, thermostat, etc.) are UL listed, but that does not mean the heaters themselves are considered safe by the UL.

If you need an exterior extension cord, chances are you're taking a risk. The UL does not recommend using an extension cord with a submersible electrical heater. To be listed UL 499, a submersible heater must have a cord of at least two feet long and no longer than six feet.

If you don't have an outside outlet, consider the risks before you plug your heater into an extension cord to an outside light socket, or drill a hole for the cord through your windowsill.

Why don't they make solar- or battery-powered heaters? While it doesn't take too much energy to convert solar or battery power to light, the power requirements of a heating system are too great for batteries or solar power.

If you decide to heat your bath, consider how much it costs to power the heater. Some heaters have thermostats that kick on only when the temperature drops below 40 degrees; others are on all winter (or until you turn them off).

One final thought: If you paint the surface of your birdbath black, you'll increase the amount of heat the bath absorbs and keep the water warmer than the air temperature.

The Nelson Blue Devil   The Smith-Gates Water Warmer

Audubon Plastics Heated Bath

Audubon Plastics sells a plastic bath on a 3-foot post, heated by a light bulb hidden under the bowl. The 16-inch bowl is 2⅛ inches deep. The heater is thermostatically controlled. The heater is not UL approved, but the parts are.

Looker Heated Bath

Looker Products has a heated version of its plastic pan bath. The bath is warmed by a thermostatically controlled heating unit hidden under the pan. The heater is not UL listed.

Ol' Sam Peabody Heated Bath

The Ol' Sam Peabody Company sells a heated bath that sits in a wooden shell of Michigan white cedar. The 1-foot-diameter bath requires a regular outside grounded utility cord.

Smith-Gates Water Warmer

The Smith-Gates Water Warmer is not technically for birdbaths. It is designed for use in the poultry industry and is UL listed. It looks like a metal test tube, and is meant for a deep (3 inches or more) bath. In accordance with UL standards, the water warmer comes with a 6-foot cord. The manufacturer and UL do not recommend using it with an extension cord. The Smith-Gates Company warranties this product for one year.

Nelson Blue Devil Heater

The Blue Devil birdbath heater is not UL listed because its cord is so short. The manufacturer says the Blue Devil is listed by the CSA (Canada's equivalent of the UL). Some consumers feel safe when they cover the plug with a plastic bag and seal it with tape. This may keep out moisture, but it's still dangerous.

Farm Innovators B-9 Heater

Farm Innovators' bath deicer is half the price of other heaters. About the size of your outstretched hand, the B-9 is little more than heat strips covered with two layers of heavy-duty aluminum foil, with a short wire and grounded plug. Designed for shallow baths, it has no thermostat and uses 40 watts. The manufacturer claims it keeps a 3-inch circle of water open at 0 degrees. When the thermometer hit 20 degrees in Heidi's front yard last February, the 2 inches of water in her bath were frozen solid. It is not UL listed, but comes with a one-year warranty.

Noisemakers

Several products are available to simulate the sound of water falling. The Drip Spout and Fountain Mist attachments are portable water units that create the sound that attracts birds while providing fresh water. They connect easily without tools to your outside house faucet. All connections are of high-quality metal.

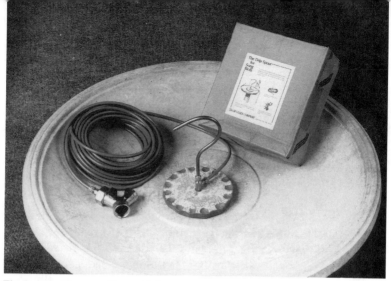

The Beverly Company Copper Drip Spout

Beverly Company Copper Drip Spout

The Copper Drip Spout is about 7 inches high, mounted on a hand-crafted glazed stoneware base. Each spout kit comes with 50 feet of miniature green plastic hose you can either bury or run along the grass to your bath.

A two-way metal Y-valve faucet attachment permits independent use of garden hose and Drip Spout. You open the outside faucet and adjust the water flow with the levers on the valve. By setting the dripper for a slow, steady drip, you may be able to balance evaporation with the drips. The more water you allow, the more chance your bath will overflow. An overflow may not be all bad. If you put your bath on a bed of rocks, the noise and motion of the water as it overflows emphasizes your water supply.

Take care when you install the Drip Spout. Don't pick it up by the hose or tighten the knurled nut (where the hose attaches to the spout) too much. The plastic sleeve inside the knurled nut can crack and break. Tighten by hand only. Replacement parts are available direct from the manufacturer. The Drip Spout comes with installation instructions. There's no warranty.

Beverly Company's Fountain Mist

Fountain Mist transforms your bath into a fountain. Except for the metal spray pedestal, this portable unit uses the same technology as the Drip Spout. Instead of the copper tube, water is forced through a tiny hole in the spray pedestal. You control the height of the mist by increasing the water flow at the Y-valve. Be patient. Give the birds some time to get used to the mist. It's a fun fountain to watch, and birds seem to like it, too. Be careful tightening the knurled nut. You don't want to break the plastic sleeves.

If your water is high in mineral content, the Fountain Mist may be more trouble than it's worth. If you notice any discoloration on the outside of the pedestal, you've got hard water. You'll have to unscrew the nozzle and washer, soak them in vinegar overnight, and scrub them with a toothbrush. Always clean the Fountain Mist before storing it for the winter. Replacement parts are available.

6

BIRDHOUSES

It seems that birds will nest just about anywhere and everywhere. A closer look at each species shows that's not quite the case. Some species—especially the louder birds, homeowners will tell you— prefer to nest right under your window.

After a century of study, ornithologists know where and how a particular bird will nest, right down to the type of tree, height above the ground, and nesting material. A glance through the *Field Guide to Birds Nests* will show you species by species where to look—in trees and shrubs, on ledges, on the ground, and in burrows.

While most birds are very particular about nest sites, the most successful species readily adapt to living around humans, nesting in some unlikely places. Starlings and house sparrows often choose traffic lights and store signs, or, more annoying, your clothes dryer or stove vent. Barn swallows may vex you by building their nests right over your front door. House finches and Carolina wrens seem to prefer hanging plant baskets. Finches are also partial to front-door lighting fixtures. And pity the poor house wren who, unknown to you, thought your outdoor gas barbecue vent looked just perfect.

So what can you do when birds nest where you don't want them? It all depends on the species, and whether the problem is a health or safety hazard or merely an annoyance. Some ornithologists suggest aggressively shooing starlings, pigeons, and sparrows. They say that you will be doing the bluebirds, chickadees, and purple martins a service.

None of these birds is native to this continent. Feisty starlings and house sparrows, because they nest in cavities, are a major cause of the decline in several native species including the bluebird. Roosting pigeons can become a serious health hazard because of their droppings.

Birds such as the house finch, barn swallow, and hawks may become backyard pests, but you may not disturb them. These birds enjoy full protection under federal law. However, if a house finch nests in your front-door lighting fixture, you could have a house fire if you don't destroy the nest.

If a pair of house finches or Carolina wrens decides to nest in the hanging basket on your deck, just ignore them and continue to water the plants. There's no reason for you to let your plants die. The finches will either stay and persevere, or abandon the nest and start over in a drier location.

The best way to get birds to nest where you want them is to learn about their requirements. Then put out houses and nesting materials. Bluebirds, for example, look for nest sites in open fields (in the middle or on the edge), and at the edge of cemeteries, golf courses, and parks. (If you have a densely wooded lot, you're not likely to attract these spectacular birds). If you have the right habitat, you can create the perfect nest site and offer nesting materials to entice them to settle in your neighborhood.

Bluebirds want a tree stump or wooden fence post with a natural cavity, or an abandoned woodpecker hole that's one and a half inches in diameter and six inches above the bottom of the cavity, with a five by five-inch floor. Simple enough? Don't despair. You can create an abandoned woodpecker nest by mounting a nesting box on a pole. Bluebirds and nearly thirty other birds will nest in boxes.

That leaves hundreds of other birds (including cardinals, finches, and orioles) who aren't interested in nesting boxes. You can still interest them in nesting nearby by considering their needs in your landscape plantings. You can also put out nesting materials (animal hairs, fiber scraps, feathers, and twigs) in the spring.

Before buying or building a nesting box, learn which birds you can support in your backyard. Not everyone has the habitat for a wood duck, purple martin, or screech owl. On the other hand, just about anyone can attract a robin, titmouse, house wren, and chickadee.

Habitat

Where you put your birdhouse is as important as its design and construction. Cavity-nesting birds are very particular about nest sites. Some must be near open water or near people. Some stick to dense woods or open fields, and some look for a combination of habitats.

It makes sense that wood ducks look for trees and water. Don't put out a box for them if you're not near a swamp, marsh, lake, pond, or stream. Tree swallows, barn swallows, phoebes, and prothonotary warblers also look for nesting sites near water.

Many birds that visit your feeders and baths will consider nesting in nearby trees. Each species, however, is looking for something just a little different. When they're not in your backyard, many birds often nest in woodland clearings. Abandoned woodpecker holes are natural nest sites for wrens, chickadees, titmice, and nuthatches.

Phoebes, barn swallows, and robins can be attracted to open-faced nest shelves mounted on trees and sides of buildings. Wrens prefer boxes hung from tree branches at about eye level. Chickadees, nuthatches, and titmice will take to boxes fastened to tree trunks.

A large lawn might catch the eye of some purple martin scouts. Your chances are even better if you're near water and a cemetery, golf course, power line right-of-way, or field. Woodland edges facing open habitat are also ideal habitats for bluebirds, kestrels, screech owls, flickers, flycatchers, and tree swallows.

Dead trees make terrific nesting sites for birds as well as habitats for other animals. If a dead tree is not endangering your house or other property, think about leaving it up because you'll encourage wildlife to stay in your yard. Should you decide to cut it down, make sure there are no nests in the branches or cavities. Autumn is the best time to remove old trees, for the birds' sake.

Houses

Remember, there's no such thing as a birdhouse that will attract just any bird. For best results, select the bird you want to see, then get a house for that particular bird.

Don't be tempted by those beautiful duplexes or houses that have more than one compartment. With the exception of purple martins, cavity-nesting birds prefer not to share a house. While these condos look great on the store shelf, starlings and house sparrows are all you're likely to see in them. Once you've decided which birds you're able to attract, go shopping. While there are hundreds of nesting boxes to choose from, some will never be right for the birds you want to see. Pay close attention to the three things that make a house right: construction materials, design, and location.

Construction Materials

It used to be that birdhouses were made of natural materials—vegetable gourds and wood. These days, you're likely to find traditional houses on shelves next to those made of terra-cotta, glazed ceramic, metal, plastic, and concrete.

The best materials are durable but not airtight. You want a house that breathes. Wood is a natural first choice. Three-quarter-inch bald cypress and red cedar are recommended. Pine and three-quarter-inch exterior-grade plywood will do, but they don't last as long.

It makes no difference whether the wood is slab, rough cut, or finished, as long as it has not been treated with a preservative. When they get hot, the chemicals in the preservatives may harm the nestlings.

You can protect your pine and plywood houses with a water-based exterior paint. Light green and tan are recommended because they're less likely to absorb heat. Galvanized or brass shank nails, hinges, and screws resist rusting and hold boxes together tightly.

Gourds are the original "disposable" birdhouses. If you grow your own, you'll have literally dozens to choose from in the years ahead. If you don't have the space to grow replacements, a coat of polyurethane (on the outside only) will add years to their life.

Designed properly, terra-cotta and glazed ceramic, metal, and plastic (polyvinyl chloride and foam) houses will breathe and are durable. The biggest problem with terra-cotta and ceramic is that when they drop, they break. Inadequate ventilation, inadequate drainage, and lack of easy access for maintenance are important concerns.

Resist the temptation to put a metal roof on your birdhouse. Reflective metal makes sense for martin houses, but it's superfluous with wooden houses, and may increase the interior temperature of the box.

And then there's Wood-Crete. These houses, made in Germany and in Tennessee, are a mix of sawdust, burnt clay, and concrete. They breathe like wood and should last two decades or more. Squirrels can't chew their way in like they can with wood, plastic, gourds, and terra-cotta.

Design

Each species has specific requirements for nest box size: diameter of entrance hole, height of hole above the box floor, box floor, box height, box depth, and placement height. Keep in mind that not every bird has read the research. It's not unusual to find birds you never expected nesting in a house you built for someone else.

For example, bluebirds have been known to nest in purple martin condos. Open a bluebird house and you may find a house sparrow, titmouse, or tree swallow. Chickadees and house wrens are always squabbling over nest boxes.

Tables 6.1 and 6.2 list specifics for many species that will nest nearby your home.

Once you've got the correct measurements, take a look at ventilation, drainage, susceptibility to predation, and ease of maintenance.

There are two ways to provide ventilation: leave gaps between the roof and sides of the box or drill half-inch holes in the sides just below the roof.

You can assure proper drainage the same way: cut away the corners of the box floor and drill half-inch holes in the floor. Look for a nest-box floor that's recessed about one-quarter inch from the bottom of box sides; that will keep rainwater from sitting on the floor.

Box depth, roof, and entrance hole design help minimize predator (raccoon, cat, opossum, and red squirrel) access. Sometimes all it takes is an angled roof with a three-inch or more overhang to discourage mammals. And all it takes to discourage blowfly larvae from emerging in the nest is a shelf of hardware cloth about one-quarter inch above the floor.

The entrance hole is the only thing between a predator and a birdhouse full of nestlings. By itself, the three-quarter-inch-thick wall isn't wide enough to keep out the arm of a raccoon or cat, or the sharp bill of a hungry kestrel. Add a predator guard, a three-quarter-inch-thick rectangular wood block, to thicken the wall, and you'll discourage sparrows, starlings, and other predators. Never buy a birdhouse with a perch at the entrance hole unless you want to attract starlings and house sparrows. These and other predators such as kestrels sit on a perch waiting for that perfect opportunity to grab the nestlings.

A rough surface on the inside of the box front panel makes it easier for the nestlings to get out of the box when it's time to fledge. If your box is made of smooth wood, just add grooves, cleats, or wire mesh.

Finally, you can make a box more attractive to wood ducks, screech owls, and woodpeckers by filling the bottom with sawdust or wood shavings.

Location

You've bought the perfect house. You put it in your backyard in March. The months pass, and not one bird has so much as landed

Table 6.1 NEST BOX DIMENSIONS

Species	Box Floor (inches)	Box Height (inches)	Entrance Height (inches)	Entrance Diameter (inches)	Placement Height (feet)
American Robin	7 × 8	8	—	—	6–15
Eastern Bluebird	4 × 4	8–12	6–10	1½	4–6
Western Bluebird*					
Mountain Bluebird	5 × 5	8–12	6–10	1½	4–6
Chickadee	4 × 4	8–10	6–8	1⅛	4–15
Titmouse	4 × 4	8–10	6–8	1¼	5–15
Ash-throated Flycatcher	6 × 6	8–10	6–8	1½	5–15
Great Crested Flycatcher	6 × 6	8–10	6–8	1¾	5–15
Phoebe†	6 × 6	6	—	—	8–12
Brown-headed Pygmy;					
Red-breasted Nuthatch	4 × 4	8–10	6–8	1¼	5–15
White-breasted Nuthatch	4 × 4	8–10	6–8	1⅜	5–15
Prothonotary Warbler	5 × 5	6	4–5	1⅜	4–8
Barn Swallow†	6 × 6	6	—	—	8–12
Purple Martin	6 × 6	6	1–2	2½	6–20
Tree and Violet-Green Swallows	5 × 5	6–8	4–6	1½	5–15
Downy Woodpecker	4 × 4	8–10	6–8	1¼	5–15
Golden-fronted Woodpecker	6 × 6	12–15	9–12	2	10–20
Hairy Woodpecker	6 × 6	12–15	9–12	1½	8–20

Species	Box Floor	Box Height	Entrance Diameter	Entrance Height	Placement Height
Lewis' Woodpecker	7×7	16–18	14–16	2½	12–20
Northern Flicker	7×7	16–18	14–16	2½	6–20
Pileated Woodpecker	8×8	16–24	12–20	3–4	15–25
Red-headed Woodpecker	6×6	12–15	9–12	2	10–20
Yellow-bellied Sapsucker	6×6	12–15	9–12	1½	10–20
Bewick's and House Wrens	4×4	6–8	4–6	1¼	5–10
Carolina Wren	4×4	6–8	4–6	—	5–12

†Use nesting shelf—a platform with three sides and an open front.
*Some studies recommend 5 × 5″ floors for all bluebirds.

SOURCE: Department of Defense, Natural Resources Program, Technical Report EL-88-19, Songbird Nest Boxes, Section 5.1.8, US Army Corps of Engineers Wildlife Resources Management Manual by Wilma Mitchell, Department of the Army, Waterways Experiment Station, 1988, Corps of Engineers, PO Box 631, Vicksburg, Mississippi 39181-0631.

Table 6.2 BOXES FOR OTHER BIRDS

SPECIES	BOX FLOOR (inches)	BOX HEIGHT (inches)	ENTRANCE DIAMETER (inches)	ENTRANCE HEIGHT (inches)	PLACEMENT HEIGHT (feet)
Barn Owl	10×18	15–18	4	6	12–18
Screech Owl, Kestrel	8×8	12–15	9–12	3	10–30
Osprey	48×48 platform only				
Red-tailed Hawk and Great Horned Owl	24×24 platform only				
Wood Duck	10×18	10–24	12–16	4	10–20

SOURCE: Homes for Birds, Conservation Bulletin #14, US Department of the Interior, Washington, DC.

on your house. What's wrong? It may be one or a combination of several things, including marginal habitat or where you put the house.

There's a lot you can do to modify your land to attract the birds you want to see. It can be as simple as putting out a birdbath or as complicated as felling trees, planting fruit-bearing plants, and installing a pond with a waterfall. But it's much easier just to identify the birds most likely to take to your backyard, and put the appropriate next box in the right place.

There's a wide range of how high and low you can place a nest box. Pick a height that's convenient for you. After all, you'll want to watch it and you have to maintain it. If you want to watch chickadees from your second-floor window or deck, fifteen feet up is not unreasonable, but it's a lot easier to clean a box placed at eye level.

Experts recommend no more than four small nest boxes and one large box per acre. Try to put about a hundred yards between bluebird boxes and seventy-five yards between tree swallow boxes. Don't put your nesting box near your feeder because you don't want to attract birds with hunger on their mind to a birdhouse with vulnerable fledglings. Baby birds are a temptation for many birds, squirrels, and other creatures. And don't put more than one box in a tree, unless the tree is extremely large.

In regions known for cold spring weather, experts recommend placing the boxes so the entrance faces southeast, or away from the prevailing winds. In areas with extremely hot summers, boxes facing prevailing winds are cooler.

Maintenance

Properly designed birdhouses are *structurally* maintenance-free. But because cavity-nesting birds are susceptible to all kinds of disruptions, responsible landlords should look in on the nests regularly. If you try to attract bluebirds, for example, evicting house sparrows and starlings may become a regular event. Be persistent. You may have to kick them out several times before they comply.

House sparrows and starlings aren't the only birds to take over bluebird boxes. When wrens, titmice, and chickadees are the culprits, you have two options: put up with them or evict them. If you evict them, consider putting up an additional nest box for them nearby.

Mice, squirrels, and insects may also compete for your nest boxes. Be careful when you inspect the boxes. Rodents aren't necessarily going to hurt you, but wasps and bees might. Look for fleas, flies, mites, larvae, and lice in the bottom of the box.

As a prophylactic against insects, consider spraying the interior of your box with 1 percent rotenone powder or a pyrethrum spray. If wasps are a problem, coat the inside top of the box with bar soap.

Clean out the nesting box after each brood has fledged. Birds may nest several times a season. But many cavity-nesting birds will not nest again in a box full of someone else's or their own nesting materials. When you don't see any bird activity near the nest, first tap on the box. If there's no noisy response, take a peek inside. Chances are good that the birds are gone and it's time for you to do your job.

Boxes with easy access make your job easy. They can be opened from the top, side, front, or bottom, but you are less likely to disturb nesting birds with a top-opening box. While the babies might jump out of the nest when you open the box from the side or front, these are the most convenient designs.

If the babies do jump out, don't panic. Just pick them up and put them back in the nest. Don't worry that the parents will smell your scent and reject their babies. That's a myth. Most birds have a terrible sense of smell.

In the fall, after you've cleaned out your nest boxes for the last time, consider storing them in the basement for the winter. That's sure to increase the life of gourds and hanging nest boxes. But don't bother to take down nest boxes nailed to tree trunks. They may provide birds and other animals with winter shelter. Each spring be sure to clean out all houses you've left out for the winter.

Wildlife Products Samson Nesting Material

Rating the Products

Nesting Materials

A friend of ours, watching a chickadee pull some cottony material from a prepackaged nesting pack, said, "Get yourself a twig!"

Birds don't need your help with actual nest building. Provide them with the right habitat and an empty birdhouse, and they'll scavenge your yard for nesting materials.

But if your yard is particularly tidy, you can offer them a mesh bag full of stuff they can use. Gather your own stuff or use the prepackaged products.

Wildlife Products Samson Nesting Material

Samson Nesting Material consists of a variety of materials including yarn, feathers, and wood. Because half the fun of offering nesting material is watching birds pick it up with their bills, you should consider placing it near your window.

Wildlife Products says its Samson Nesting Material is "proven to increase birds by astonishing numbers and hold them in your yard." We're not sure what these astonishing numbers are, but the two packets of sterilized feathers, moss, hair, string, and cotton are the matter more than fifty birds use to make their nests. And each box contains enough for two dozen nests.

Be sure to spend some time reading the bright red box. It's packed with tips on how to attract birds, including the suggestion that you "have some mud on hand for the robins because, as you know, they line their nests with it."

You get a full money-back guarantee with Samson.

Havegard Farm Best Nest Builder

If it's goldfinches you're after, Havegard Farm has a nesting product for you. Best Nest Builder is little more than a sterilized wad of cotton, about the size of a baseball, packed into a string mesh hanger.

The cotton simulates natural thistle down, the stuff finches collect in August to line their nests. Put one of these near your thistle feeder, and you may entice wild canaries to build in your yard.

Predator Guards

Predator guards are usually plastic contraptions that permit birds to enter birdhouses but keep other animals out.

Audubon Entities Bird Guardian

Audubon Entities, a Midwest manufacturer, has created a retrofit tunnel that resembles a plastic hair curler from the 1960s. Just snap the Bird Guardian into any 1½-inch entrance hole, and you can increase its depth by about three inches. The Guardian will either keep predators out, or give them a perch to sit on—we're not sure which. Contact the North American Bluebird Society for the results of their field tests. The society's recommendations were not available when this book went to press.

Havegard Farm Best Nest Builder   A small-bird house by Dave Eastman

Wooden and Concrete Houses

Country Ecology Birdhouses

Most of Country Ecology's houses are made of weathered New Hampshire white pine with bark slab fronts. Dave Eastman gets his material at the local sawmill, then constructs the smaller birdhouses so they look like natural tree cavities. Eastman's wood duck and kestrel or owl houses are made with weathered gray pine board front panels. These pine houses are not likely to last as long as cedar houses, but they're well built and very attractive.

The thick slab bark panels on the smaller birdhouses act as natural predator guards. They're securely fastened with a galvanized box screw. Loosen the screw and the front flips out for easy nest cleaning.

Eastman pays careful attention to the correct measurements, drainage, and ventilation for each species. There are Eastman birdhouses available for a wide range of species including bluebird, tree swallow, chickadee, downy woodpecker, titmouse, nuthatch, wren, wood duck, kestrel, and screech owl. The houses come with full instructions.

Arthur C. Brown Birdhouses

The Arthur C. Brown Company distributes a complete line of ¾-inch western red cedar houses. Designed with the cooperation of the National Audubon Society, the dimensions are correct for each species.

When you purchase one of these houses check the sides for vent holes and bottoms for drainage. You will have to drill some holes. Only the wood duck and bluebird boxes have flip-out fronts for easy access. The other boxes are accessible through a push-up bottom, making it difficult to determine when they're vacant or need cleaning.

The cedar bluebird house and feeder, with its flip-out front panel and built-in predator guard, is the company's best product. It's based on a design by Jack Finch, a former director of the North American Bluebird Society. With the front panel up, it's a house. The cardboard nesting cup makes maintenance easier. Slide the panel down, and it's a feeder. A small piece of wood on top of the nesting cup makes a tray for Miracle Meal, raisins, peanut hearts, and holly or dogwood berries. Complete with a galvanized three-section pole, it's a great buy.

New on the birdhouse shelves is Brown's handwoven nest for birds of prey. Placed securely in an old dead tree, this 32-inch diameter, black rattan basket imported from Indonesia may attract a red-tail hawk, osprey, or great horned owl. The company manufactures housing for bluebirds, tree swallows, chickadees, downy woodpeckers, titmice, nuthatches, wrens, wood ducks, kestrels, screech owls, robins, barn swallows, and flickers. All of these houses come with complete instructions.

The Arthur C. Brown Bluebird House

The Schwelger birdhouse with predator guards

The Schwelger barn swallow nest

Schwelger Birdhouses

Over 6 million Schwelger birdhouses sit in gardens, vineyards, and forests all over Europe. These West German imports, made from a unique mix of sawdust and concrete, breathe like natural wood. But unlike most wooden houses, these Wood-Crete homes are rot and squirrel proof, and will last twenty years or more.

Their gray front panels are interchangeable and removable for easy inspection and cleaning. The three hanging models are quite stable in the wind, since they weigh eight pounds. The six tree- or building-mounted models come complete with nails and hangers.

The two predator-proof models have built-in plastic guards inside the entrance. Our only concern is how the fledglings manage to climb over the predator guard? The small holes below the entrance are supposed to add to their protection by coaxing birds to nest farther back in the box, away from the light, out of easy reach of predators.

Some of these houses lack drainage holes; none has air vents. Schwelger birdhouses are built for the following species: bluebird, tree swallow, chickadee, downy woodpecker, titmouse, nuthatch, wren, wood duck, kestrel, screech owl, barn swallow, flicker, house finch, purple martin, and great crested flycatcher.

The instructions are complete, although some of the information on their yellow wrapper is at odds with a U.S. government report on birdhouses. Schwelger says the "type of landscape does not influence the number of birdhouses that can be placed. In the yard and garden, houses can be mounted on every other tree, if there are no birdhouses in the neighbor's yard." This is not a good idea. The instructions are incomplete in that they recommend "cleaning out old nests every year, usually late summer or fall. This helps to control parasites." You should clean out the nest box when each brood has fledged.

Greenpath Birdhouses

If you like houses that are attractive, take a look at the Greenpath log- and acorn-style houses for small birds. The manufacturer says these birdhouses will not crack, split, rot, rust or decay.

These waterproof houses also breathe, and added drainage and ventilation holes prevent water accumulation and overheating. The exterior has a natural bark pattern. The interior has a rough finish. Top opening, they are easy to clean but somewhat difficult to monitor. They will survive the winter weather, but they are not unbreakable. Consider bringing them in for the winter.

Greenpath birdhouses are built for bluebird, tree swallow, chickadee, downy woodpecker, titmouse, nuthatch, and wren. The houses come with complete instructions.

Birdhouses by Greenpath

Cousin Dan Birdhouses

If you're looking for cute, take a look at the apples, acorns, pears, and mini-beehives made by Cousin Dan. But don't buy them. Varnished inside and out, the solid pine houses are durable, waterproof, and airtight. In fact, nestlings may have a difficult time keeping cool and escaping when it's time to fledge.

If you can't resist buying one, add drainage holes and air vents. Throw away the perch because it gives easy access for predators.

The roof of the acorn house can be unscrewed for periodic maintenance. The apple, pear, and beehive houses have a removable plastic plug at the bottom. Cousin Dan houses are designed for chickadees, nuthatches, and wrens. They come with minimal instructions.

Marsh Creek and Bruce Barber Birdhouses

If you want attractive and functional birdhouses, take a look at the Marsh Creek and Bruce Barber western cedar houses. Both manufacturers—Charlie Rouse, a carpenter, and Bruce Barber, a

138

A birdhouse by Cousin Dan

cabinetmaker—pay close attention to detail. Their houses provide easy access (with flip-out front, top, or sides), recessed floors, grooved front panels, ventilation, and drainage.

Rouse's houses are made from rough-cut cedar; Barber's are kiln-dried finished western red cedar. Both men include complete information about how to attract each bird and how to maintain the house. They are among the best-built houses on the market today.

Marsh Creek houses are designed for wrens, chickadees, bluebirds, owls, kestels, and bats.

Bruce Barber makes houses for wrens, bluebirds, and purple martins.

Avia Observation Birdhouse

When you put out a birdhouse, sooner or later you'll find yourself wanting to take a peek at what's going on inside. Go ahead and peak. Monitoring the box is part of being a good landlord.

The Charlie Rouse Winter
Songbird Roost

A screech owl house by
Marsh Creek

A bluebird box by Marsh Creek

A wren house by Bruce Barber

The Avia Observation
Bird House

A wren house by Woodline

It's nearly impossible to monitor houses with bottom access, since the nests are likely to fall out when you open the box. That's not as much of a problem with houses that open on the front, top, or sides. In fact, easy accessibility for monitoring is a sign of a quality nest box. Avia makes a side-opening nest box they call the Observation Bird House. It's nothing more than a bluebird box with a sliding 4-inch plastic inner wall.

We had to call the company to find out what the plastic's for. The manufacturer put it there to keep the nest from falling out. It's totally unnecessary.

The Observation Bird House is made of ¾-inch eastern white pine treated with a preservative and put together with staples. What do we like about this house? Not much. It's properly vented at the top and has ample drainage holes in the floor. It could use a recessed floor, an additional 2-inch overhang on the roof, and a better mounting system.

141

Cedarline Birdhouses

These relatively inexpensive houses are made of Michigan white cedar stained gray. Most are stapled, some are nailed. Ventilation and drainage are adequate.

Woodline Birdhouses

These charming walnut-stained bluebird houses and chickadee or wren cottages offer a choice of red or green roof. The bluebird house opens at the front, the chickadee-wren house at the bottom. Don't expect them to last more than a couple of years unless you bring them in for the winter.

Recycled Paper Birdhouses

Recycled soda bottles as feeders are one thing, but recycled paper houses? We just had to see for ourselves. We first got wind of these paper houses when we saw their advertisement in the *Audubon* magazine last spring: "Durable birdhouses made from molded recycled paper. Designed to last for years even in the harshest climate. Two sizes—good for wrens to kestrels."

It's hard to imagine a birdhouse for under $5. The material resembles the cardboard cartons eggs used to come in. While there are no ventilation holes, there is one drainage hole in the bottom. It's as big as the entrance hole. Whether it will last for years is another question. We're still testing.

Pottery Birdhouses

You can hardly go to a craft fair these days without seeing a pottery birdhouse. They're usually made of stoneware terra-cotta or glazed ceramic. First look for an attractive house, then look at how well it meets the birds' needs.

Most pottery houses come with a perch. If you can, remove it. Next look for proper dimensions, drainage holes at the bottom, ventilation holes in the sides near the top, rough (unglazed) interior, and easy access for cleaning. (See chapter 7, Birdhouse Beautiful, for more examples of pottery birdhouses.)

Bennington Birdhouses

Bennington Potters has created an attractive terra-cotta wren house that looks like a small orange globe (cut in half) with a bird on top. An aluminum hanger holds the two halves together and makes hanging the house easy.

To clean or inspect the house, just slide the top up the hanger arms. The house comes with a rustic grapevine perch; toss it out. There's nothing you can do to fix the ventilation and drainage, short of a masonry drill, so hang the house in the shade where it's not likely to get much sun or rain.

These houses make homes for wrens and chickadees, and perhaps a house sparrow. Houses don't come with instructions.

Williamsburg Houses

"In Colonial Williamsburg, even the birdhouses are historically accurate," so says the promotional material accompanying the bottle birdhouses handcrafted at Williamsburg Pottery Factory. The clay birdhouses are modeled after the eighteenth-century earthenware pots excavated by archaeologists at Colonial Williamsburg.

The twentieth-century versions are made from a local clay coated with a transparent glaze to make them waterproof and warm.

These orange-colored vase-shaped "pots" with holes in the bottom are meant to be hung from a nail. Pick a spot that gets morning sun and afternoon shade, about five feet up on the side of your house, fence, garage, or tree. Don't add a perch, as the manufacturer recommends; if you do, all you're likely to attract are house sparrows and starlings.

Ventilation is not a problem, but drainage is. The Pottery people assured us they will add adequate drainage holes.

These houses are built for wrens. The instructions come with interesting historical information, but no advice on attracting wild birds.

Opus Birdhouses

Opus manufactures an attractive two-piece terra-cotta wren house with a carved tile roof. The house could use two more drainage

The Bennington Potters
Terra-Cotta Wren House

A Colonial Williamsburg clay
bottle

The Opus Terra-Cotta
Wren House

holes and three vent holes just under the roof. But the dimensions
are what the U.S. Fish and Wildlife Service recommends. You don't
need the cute perch, so give it the heave-ho. Then figure out where
you want the house—hanging or bracket mounted.

Either way, it's not as simple as the packaging implies. The two
short plastic ropes are frustrating. They're supposed to hold the roof
to the base, hang the house, and keep it from spinning. If you're
worried about the house spinning in the wind, it's a lot easier to
use metal wire. It's nearly impossible to get a knot to hold using
the slick plastic rope.

If you'd rather mount the house to a wall or tree with a bracket,
the manufacturer suggests you glue Velcro tabs (they're in the box)
to the roof and base. The instructions suggest using Krazy Glue.
Good luck.

Opus terra-cotta houses are built for house, Carolina, and winter
wrens. The houses come with complete installation instructions,
however it's not clear why the instruction sheet includes a birdfeeding chart. Birdhouses should not be confused with feeders, nor
placed near them.

Carruth Studio Kitty Wren House

Another Carruth Kitty product! Wrens will nest in this house and there's nothing like watching a bird fly into the cat's mouth. Unfortunately, this wren house isn't designed to protect birds from predators, so mount it in a safe place such as on top of a post. A baffle below would be a good idea, too.

Creatively Designed Birdhouses

Creatively Designed Products' stoneware birdhouses could easily be mistaken for gnomes' homes. Wrens and chickadees will find the peaked, vented-roof, hanging home quite attractive. But the perch and the generous entrance hole are not well thought out. CDP is currently making improvements. The houses will attract wrens and chickadees. There are no instructions with the house.

Natural Gourd Houses

Native Americans discovered how to attract bug zappers—birds that eat insects—hundreds of years ago. They hung hollowed-out gourds around their villages to house birds that eat insect pests.

If you travel through the southern states, you're likely to see, hanging from wires and poles, gourds full of purple martins. More recently, northerners also have discovered that cavity-nesting birds nest in gourds.

Home Grown Houses

You can pick up birdhouse, or calabash, gourd seeds at most garden centers. But if you don't have the inclination, the sun, or the space, Home Grown Houses will do the job for you. Each year Lynn Leatherman and his crew transform thousands of gourds into housing for wrens, chickadees, titmice, bluebirds, and purple martins. The gourds are grown in Georgia and shipped north to Home Grown Houses in West Virginia. They're sorted according to size,

The Carruth Studio Kitty Wren House

A stoneware birdhouse by Creatively
Designed Products

A gourd birdhouse by Home Grown Houses

cleaned, and coated with polyurethane. Leatherman's crew drills the entrance hole, holes in the top for hangers and vents, and holes in the base for drainage.

All you have to do is hang them from a tree or, in the case of the purple martin gourds, string them from a wire or attach them to the base of your wood or aluminum martin house. Gourd houses are an attractive alternative martin house because starlings and house sparrows don't seem to like them. These two pest birds prefer houses that have perches and don't swing in the wind.

Home Grown Houses are available for purple martins, wrens, owls, woodpeckers, chickadees, titmice, and bluebirds.

Birdhouse Kits

Several companies manufacture birdhouse kits, primarily for children to put together with the aid of an adult. With the exception of Marsh Creek's, most kits could stand some improvement in design, instructions, or materials.

Woodkrafter Kits

Woodkrafter manufactures kits for chickadee, bluebird, and wren houses. All are made of precut, predrilled cedar. All you need is a hammer, a screwdriver, and some time; no finishing is required. It may well be, as the packaging claims, that these products meet Audubon Society specifications. We'd rather see houses that meet the U.S. Fish and Wildlife Service specifications. The kits could use additional drainage and vent holes, recessed floors, easier access for monitoring, and a coat of exterior latex paint.

Marsh Creek Kits

The only difference between the houses Marsh Creek sells assembled and those in kit form is the wood and the laborer. Charlie Rouse assembles ¾-inch western red cedar houses. He cuts the same houses in pine for you to assemble. Just add a coat of exterior latex and you have one of the best birdhouses on the market.

A birdhouse built from the Mill Store Products kit

The Bird Abode built from the Channelcraft kit

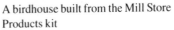

Mill Store Kits

Mill Store Products manufactures two ½-inch pine kits, the Alpine and Studio houses. Both come with instructions which include a parts list. Both have screw panels for (not-so) easy access.

The two kits have design problems: no drainage holes, no recessed floor, and short roof overhangs. Both could benefit from predrilled screw and nail holes to eliminate wood splitting. The Studio kit could do with about an inch more on both ends of the back panel and the bottom of the front panel.

These houses are designed for chickadees and wrens. The kits come with assembly instructions, but with no information about where to put the houses and which birds might be attracted to them.

Channelcraft Bird Abode Kit

Channelcraft's Bird Abode kit is one of the most attractive packages on the market. All the pieces are sanded. All the nail holes are predrilled. The kit comes with more than enough nails.

148

As handsome as the finished product is, it's plagued by serious design problems: no ventilation, no drainage, no recessed floor, no ready access for monitoring or cleaning (no screws or hinges), odd dimensions (twice as deep as high, perfect for sparrows), and an odd lip below the entrance hole (an invitation to predators).

If you plan to give this kit to your children, talk them through it. There are no assembly instructions and no parts list—only a diagram of parts.

The manufacturer offers some information on which birds might visit this house based on entrance-hole size preferences, but even that is very general. The house is for house wrens and chickadees.

Purple Martin Houses

Housing for purple martins deserves special mention because it's so expensive. Don't buy or build a martin house before you understand exactly what you're getting into.

An easy way to start is at the library or local nature center. *The Purple Martin*, by R. B. Layton, and *Attracting Purple Martins*, by J. L. Wade, are two books you'll want to read. Consider a subscription to the *Purple Martin Update,* a quarterly written by James Hill's Purple Martin Conservation Association, and *Nature Society News,* a monthly tabloid full of anecdotal observations, sponsored by Nature House, J. L. Wade's martin house company.

The purple martin is North America's largest swallow. Colonial nesters, martins who visit the East Coast depend on humans to house them in the warm months. They spend the winter in Brazil and follow a predictable schedule as they migrate north each spring.

Martins are sought after tenants because of their reputations for eating thousands of insects each day.

And, yes, martins do eat enormous numbers of flying insects. But, alas, according to noted ornithologist George Miksch Sutton, and contrary to Nature House's aphorism "a purple martin can eat up to 2,000 mosquitoes a day," purple martins don't live up to their reputation as mosquito killers.

In his book *Fifty Common Birds of Oklahoma and the Southern Great Plains*, Sutton wrote, "Martins must surely catch some mosquitoes along with gnats, midges, craneflies, and the like, but the mosquitoes just happen to be caught. Expending much energy on capturing such small fry would be poor economy. . . . One insect to which they turn often is the dragonfly, a creature that does eat mosquitoes. The martin that eats one dragonfly may, in a sense, be saving the lives of scores, perhaps hundreds, of mosquitoes."

If you're looking for mosquito control, try a bat house. If you're looking for an entertaining neighbor, a purple martin colony fills the bill. But don't put up a martin condo before you've evaluated your chances of attracting these birds. Even then, there is no guarantee martins will move in.

First, decide whether you have the right habitat. If yours is a wooded lot with no natural water source nearby, chances are slim. They need about forty feet of open space on all sides of the house.

If you have the right habitat and neighbors with active martin colonies, your chances are excellent. The next question is which house is best? That depends on how much effort you're willing to put into being a landlord, what looks good to you, and the price you're willing to pay.

Plastic gourds are a good buy. They're relatively inexpensive and require minimal effort for installation and maintenance. Natural gourds are a close second. If you use untreated gourds, drill a half-dozen holes and string them up. You may want to coat the gourds with white exterior latex house paint or leave them natural, with a coat of polyurethane to add to their durability.

Gourds may have an additional advantage: starlings and house sparrows, don't seem to like them. The starlings and house sparrows that visit the millet feeder in Heidi's yard have never so much as landed on the martin gourds just twenty feet away. It may be that these alien birds are deterred by the swaying.

An aluminum house in a ready-to-assemble kit is expensive. Plan on spending part of a weekend installing it. Once you get the ground socket anchored in concrete, the telescoping poles make it easy to access the houses for regular maintenance. Aluminum houses are easy to clean and should last decades.

Wooden houses are often the most expensive. They are very heavy (over twenty pounds) and require a sturdy pole and considerable end-of-season maintenance.

No matter which material is used, a martin condo has to measure up to what the birds require: entrance hole diameter and location, compartment size, and house placement.

Purple martins look for big rooms—six-inch cubes, or preferably larger. They prefer an entrance hole two and a half inches in diameter, raised about one and a half inches above the floor.

Martin houses sit in direct sun all day, so proper ventilation is crucial. Look for houses with vent holes and gaps at the top of each compartment and a peaked, vented roof. A white or silver roof will reflect the hot sun. Look for several drainage holes in each floor.

Some martin houses come with porches, railings, porch dividers (walls separating the porches), and roof perches. Martins like to hang out near their nest boxes. Porches and roof perches provide a convenient place for adults to mingle. Porch dividers help prevent male porch dominance, a problem when a nesting male dominates an entire floor, keeping other pairs from using adjoining compartments. Porch railings provide a perch for adults. It is a myth that railings are a barrier to keep fledglings from accidentally falling to the ground. Juveniles are more likely pushed from the house by more aggressive adults; railings won't stop them.

Once you've selected your martin house, your next problem is how to mount it. Martins prefer houses about twelve to twenty feet off the ground.

There are three ways to mount an aluminum house for easy maintenance and inspection: on a telescoping pole, on a one-piece pole with a winch, or on a one-piece pole with a pulley. If you have upper body strength, a telescoping pole is a good buy. Winches and pulleys require less strength.

Consider mounting your pole in a ground socket (a three-foot tube.) Anchor it in concrete. That keeps the house from pulling the pole out of the ground in high winds or soggy soil. It also allows you to move the martin house and pole.

The safest way to mount a wooden house is on a sturdy pole. A one and a half-inch metal pipe with a flange or a wooden 4 by 4 can be attached to pivot hinges at the ground.

Gourds can be mounted three ways: on a sturdy pole with a T at the top (and a series of pulleys), on a lightweight aluminum pole, or strung from a thick wire suspended between two poles.

As with most houses, predators can be a problem. It's hard to imagine, but cats, snakes, raccoons, and squirrels can climb up most poles and take an entire martin colony for lunch. Don't wait for it to happen; install a predator guard on the pole.

Rating the Products

Nature House Martin Houses

J. L. Wade's Nature House is the company that pioneered the aluminum purple martin house industry. It all began about twenty years ago when Nature House developed the Trio line of martin houses. With the exception of porch dividers, Nature House products offer the following:

- durable aluminum with baked white enamel paint
- telescoping poles for easy maintenance (ground sockets are available accessories)
- hinged doors for easy cleaning
- guard rails
- winter door stops to keep sparrows and starlings from setting up nests
- proper ventilation with cool white and "natural" aluminum surfaces for heat reflection

The Trio-Musselman house is available in kit form. It has just about everything except porch dividers. You cannot add floors. We recommend the heavy-duty galvanized steel telescoping MPQ pole with this house. The three-piece MPQ has easy-to-use quick-lock clamps and can withstand winds of up to 85 mph.

The twelve-compartment house weighs thirteen pounds; the six-compartment version weighs eight and a half pounds.

Nature House purple martin houses

The Trio Musselman

The Trio Grandma

The Trio Grandpa

The Trio Castle

The four-story Trio-Castle has twenty-four compartments. Don't consider it unless you're confident the birds are there. The kit includes a galvanized pole, winch and steel cable, door stops, and removable Dri-nest subfloors.

The twelve-compartment Trio-Grandpa kit (with pole, Dri-nest subfloors, and door stops) is one of the easiest aluminum houses to maintain and use. Install the pole and the house rises and lowers like a flag.

The Trio-Grandma kit (with pole) is the eight-compartment economy version of the preceding.

Nature House Duracraft

Nature House has another line of what they call "low-price" aluminum houses—the Duracraft line. Both have mounting brackets for the DP-14 telescoping post or any pipe up to 1½ inches in diameter. Door stops are not included.

The Hex (DH-12) is a twelve-room, six-sided house with easy-to-open "spring pop" doors. One major advantage to this system is the availability of add-on floor kits (DHK-6). You can increase the size of your "castle" up to twenty-four compartments (four floors) before wind resistance becomes a problem. You can also add a "star perch" to the Hex roof.

The economy model in this line, the "Box" (DR-12), is less attractive. The two-story, twelve-compartment house has a flat roof. That makes interior temperature more of a concern.

Once you get your colony going, you will be happy to know that Nature House has two additional products you may want: the spare-o-door (SD-1) and sparrow trap (ST-1). If you allow house sparrows and starlings to use your martin house, their mere presence is likely to slow down or stop the growth of your martin colony. The spare-o-door temporarily replaces a regular Trio house door. It looks like a regular door and requires no bait. A red signal tells when the trap is sprung. A special device allows you to remove the birds without opening the door.

The heavy-gauge galvanized-wire sparrow trap mounts right on your pole. Just put in some bait (bread) and wait for the pesky little house sparrows to find it.

Heath Martin Houses

The Heath Company manufactures two martin houses: an aluminum hexagonal design and a redwood model.

The aluminum house is available in four sizes: Six-, twelve-, eighteen-, and twenty-four rooms. The twelve-room house weighs only eight pounds.

The major problem with these houses is cleaning. The only access is through snap-out floors. Even if you have a single-story house, it can be a problem. When you open the floor to monitor the room, the nest can fall out. Porch railings are an option; dividers are not available.

Think about the wisdom of the plastic mounting plate. It is held to the pole with only one set screw. Heath also sells two telescoping poles with ground sockets, one without a flange for the aluminum house and one with a plastic mounting plate for the wooden houses.

Coates Martin Houses

The Purple Martin Conservation Association calls these houses "the best martin house value on the market today—the perfect starter house for the budget conscious landlord." The Coates kits are two-story, four-compartment condos. These units feature porch dividers, guard rails, peaked and ventilated roof, door plugs, hinged doors, a telescoping 12-foot pole, and an optional two-story "add-a-unit." They have all the "bells and whistles" you'll get with the more expensive models, so if you don't need a deluxe model, this one's for you.

Cool Com Martin Houses

These are preassembled stainless-steel houses, coated with acrylic enamel paint and with a foam-insulated roof. The trim is available in six colors. They have snap-lock latches, a 13-foot telescoping pole, and add-a-floor units.

Mac Industries Martin Houses

Mac manufactures plastic martin houses with very narrow porches and red roofs. They look like little Pizza Hut restaurants.

Feathers Friends Martin Houses

The Friends makes martin condos that look like they're right out of King Arthur's court. Their PVC plastic tube houses look like mini-castles. Ventilation may be a problem.

Milwaukee Pulp Products Martinium

Milwaukee Pulp Products uses a molded high-density expanded polystyrene plastic that resembles Styrofoam for their inexpensive, circular two-story house. Unlike any martin house we've seen, the entrance holes are on the top of each floor. The porches are extremely narrow and without railings. The Martinium mounts on any pipe or tubing from 1½ to 2 inches in diameter, using only a screwdriver to tighten two hose clamps.

Barber Cedar Martin Houses

Most of the martin houses in use today are made of wood. They're certainly more attractive than the metal variety. Before you build or buy one, consider how you'll get to it to clean it out when the sparrows and starlings arrive. Often twice the weight of their aluminum counterparts, mounting and maintaining a wooden house can be a hassle.

But if you have to have one and don't want to build it yourself, let Bruce Barber do it for you. His two-story, eight-room western cedar martin houses are spectacular.

The birds are likely to appreciate his attention to detail, too. The houses come complete with screened attics, porches with railings, porch dividers, and oversized compartments. At the end of each season, Barber recommends adding a coat of boiled linseed oil to the exterior and cleaning or disinfecting the interior chambers with bleach.

Barber makes an accessory worthy of mention: the starling-house sparrow nest box trap. The trap is exactly what it sounds like—a trap that looks like a nest box. It needs no bait. The offensive birds, lured by the promise of a nest site, trip the entrance door shut. But monitor the box daily, and leave it in the shut position when you're not around.

A cedar martin house by
Bruce Barber

Plastic gourd houses built from the
Carrol Industries kit

Home Grown Martin Houses

Home Grown Houses manufactures martin house gourds that can
be strung from a wire or hung from a Carroll Industries' aluminum
pole with dowels. Eight or more inches in diameter, these natural
houses come with predrilled entrance holes, drainage holes, and
holes for hanging.

Cleaned and coated with polyurethane, the natural gourds should
last three or four seasons. There are no instructions.

Carroll Industries Plastic Gourd Martin House Kits

If you don't have a green thumb or want a gourd to last a lifetime,
Carroll Industries has something for you: plastic gourd kits. For
under $50, you can get a six-pack of "off-white," 8-inch-diameter
gourds. Undo a screw and the two-piece, snap-together houses separate for easy cleaning.

Be careful while putting the system together; these plastic gourds oreak if you drop them. But you can hang them from a wire, a T-bar, or from Carroll's custom 16-foot aluminum pole (complete with dowels). We recommend using a 3-foot PVC plastic tube for a ground socket. The system comes with complete instructions and a three-year warranty against breakage owing to weathering.

Heath Redwood Martin House

The Heath Company manufactures a redwood martin house with Masonite room dividers and floors. For cleaning, the roof lifts off and room dividers and floors lift out.

They are very heavy; twelve compartments weigh in at nineteen pounds; the eighteen-compartment house is twenty-four pounds. These houses could do with porch railings, porch dividers, and additional vents just below the roof.

7

BIRDHOUSE AND BIRDFEEDER BEAUTIFUL

Let's face facts. Birds are beautiful. Many birdfeeders and houses are not. Quality feeders, houses, and baths are often designed with function, not form, in mind. Some designers try so hard to keep squirrels off, rain out, bugs away, and yet let birds in that there's no imagination left for making the contraption look pleasing—or at least something you'd want in your yard. Configurations of plastic and sheet metal are pulled and twisted into nearly impossible shapes, with surfaces meeting at curious angles as if the feeders were built by a Frank Lloyd Wright.

These feeders and houses work—at least they usually let birds in and seed out when they're supposed to—but they often aren't much to look at. They don't go with tulips, sculptured bushes, or a trimmed lawn. Admit it, some feeders are fairly ugly looking, especially after a squirrel's munched them or a flock of finches have messed them up.

And while we're on this path of honesty, let's acknowledge the whole truth: one of the reasons we feed birds is that they look nice. We don't really feed birds because it's good for them; bird feeding is good for *us*. That's why we got into this hobby. So why muck things up with unpleasant houses and feeders?

There are some beautiful feeders and houses that will comple-

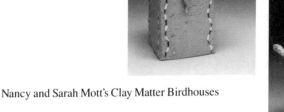

Nancy and Sarah Mott's Clay Matter Birdhouses

ment your landscaping and gardens. Believe us, these feeders and houses are a lot better looking than those pink flamingos.

Some of these feeders and houses are works of art—in fact, collectors buy them as art. Nancy and Sarah Mott's birdhouses easily fall into this category. We first saw them in the Washington, D.C., home of Randy Rosenberg, an art dealer. There's no question that they can really make your yard look terrific.

Unlike most feeders and houses we've evaluated, we don't go into detail about these products because people buy them primarily for the way they look, not the way they perform. And we don't compare their relative beauty. Suffice it to say that if a particular feeder or birdhouse made it into this chapter, it's a magnificent object.

Birdhouses by Richard Clark
(also top two next page)

A screech owl house

The Zen Temple

A flicker house

A hairy woodpecker house

The Large Oriental birdfeeder

A barn owl house

The Taunton Bird Feeder

The Wilecombe Dovecote

8

DIVERSIONARY FEEDERS

Mention the word "birdfeeder" to health officials, and you may provoke a lecture about why feeding birds is not a good idea. They'll tell you about how rats and birdfeeders go together. (And you'll tell them the mixed birdseed story.) They'll tell you about food-borne diseases like salmonella. (And you'll tell them about how you clean your feeders regularly with bleach.) Frustrated, they will tell you about squirrels.

As we've mentioned, squirrels will be a problem if you're unwilling to compromise feeder placement and esthetics. What we haven't mentioned is that some people who don't want to compromise have kept squirrels at bay by feeding them.

These people recognize that squirrels are cute. They think squirrels are fun to watch. Some tell us they know many squirrels who think they are birds. They tell stories of how squirrels try to fly to feeders and eat as much birdseed as they can. The reasoning is that if you set aside a feeder for squirrels, raccoons, and other non-feathered critters, you're likely to have more birdseed left for the birds.

The next section describes some feeders for squirrels or other wildlife. We suggest you place them far away from your birdfeeders.

Rating the Products

Squirrel Feeders

Wildlife Diversion Feeder

This rather ugly little metal feeder by Nelson Products performs its task well. The bin holds several pounds of squirrel food, depending on what you put in it: peanut kernels, peanuts in the shell, corn, striped sunflower, cats (only kidding), even chocolate. You can mix food to give your squirrels a gourmet variety snack, but if you do you'll discover that squirrels, like birds, have very clear preferences. Squirrels paw through the trough to get at what they want—say peanuts—and spill the remainder over the side. In other words, squirrels make a mess. But it's probably better that they make a mess at their own feeder than at your birdfeeder or in your tulip bed.

The squirrel feeder is made of galvanized steel, which means that a squirrel's teeth will give out before the feeder does. The feeder can be mounted on a tree trunk or wooden pole, or attached to a fence with the bracket holes on back. Refill it simply by lifting the top and pouring the feed in. A metal awning covers the trough to keep the seed dry.

Looks aren't the squirrel feeder's high points, but the most common site is in a distant part of the yard away from the birdfeeders. What is important is that the feeder is easy for squirrels to get to, so they're likely to leave your other feeders alone.

Wildwood Farms Duet Diner

You'll have to excuse the stuffed squirrels in the picture, but the manufacturer (who supplied this photo) apparently got tired of waiting for squirrels to pose properly. We can't say we blame him. What can you really say about the Duet Diner? You don't need it to feed squirrels, but it's fun. Squirrels seem to enjoy it. They may not sit so politely on the little stools, but they will put on a good show.

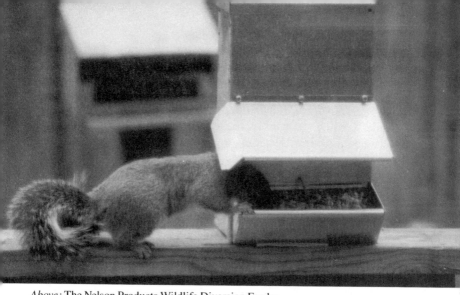

Above: The Nelson Products Wildlife Diversion Feeder

Below: The Wildwood Farms Duet Diner

And when they've finished the corn, they may start eating the feeder itself.

Wildwood Farms specializes in manufacturing squirrel paraphernalia, including food and feeders. While some avid birdlovers may consider feeding squirrels as feeding the enemy, we look at it this way: when a squirrel visits his own feeder, he isn't bothering the feeder for the birds. Put differently, a well-fed squirrel makes for a happy birdwatcher.

Corncob Chain

Go to the hardware store and buy an eye screw, some chain, and an S hook. Then buy some field corn. What could be simpler? Well, several manufacturers are confident you'd rather not put it together yourself. Chances are, you'll find a selection of squirrel corn chains waiting for you when you pick up corn.

Corn Feeder

Here's another fun way to feed squirrels. The Corn Feeder can be attached to a tree or mounted on a platform. Replacing old cobs is easy. By the way, hungry squirrels will consume a cob of corn in an afternoon. Dozens of companies manufacture corn feeders.

Squirrel Throne

Several manufacturers have introduced a variation of this chair and table feeder (we call it the "throne"). The major drawback with the squirrel throne is that squirrels might take this product seriously.

Multi-Cob Feeder or Squirrel Pole

This is guaranteed to attract squirrels. Wildwood Farms manufactures this feeder.

A corncob chain

The Corn Feeder

The Squirrel Throne

The Wildwood Farms Multi-Cob Feeder

The Wildwood Farms Corn and Seed Feeder

Wildwood Farms Corn and Seed Feeder

Why anybody would want a feeder that trains squirrels to eat from birdfeeders is beyond us. However, if you absolutely want to feed squirrels, or you want to create a very attractive squirrel diversion, this is the feeder of choice. Of course, you may have a curious problem with this feeder: how do you keep hungry flocks of doves away?

Wildlife Products Squirrel-a-Whirl

Squirrel aficionados may think this feeder is cruel. Squirrels don't seem to mind entertaining us and themselves on this prop. All you need is a tree, post, or fence on which to mount it. It's 36 inches long, and comes complete with wooden arms and a mounting bracket.

We've never seen three squirrels at a time, and it's not a likely occurrence. However, the three ears of corn mean that you don't have to retrieve used ears too often. Whirling squirrel feeders are among the most amusing contraptions you can put in a yard.

Use wood glue when you put the feeder together. Squirrels have been known to pull off the corn, spokes and all. Another tip: break the corn in half. Bolt the corn to the feeder via the stake screw.

Squirrel Houses

Some people like to test the anti-squirrel capabilities of their feeders vigorously by hosting families of squirrels in their yard. All it really takes is one birdfeeder to do the trick—where squirrels find food, they will build their own nests (called dreys). But if you want to encourage a squirrel to stay, just put up one of these squirrel boxes and you will have happy families of squirrels permanently housed nearby.

If you have problems with squirrels taking up residence in your attic—or worse, your birdhouses—putting up a squirrel house may be your only way of coaxing them out.

The Wildlife Products Squirrel-a-Whirl

A squirrel house

9

POLES

A pole is a pole, right? Not a big decision here. Well, it's not quite that simple. Some poles are better than others.

The first question is, where do you want your feeder? Set in the ground by your window? On your patio or deck? Hanging from your windowframe?

If you plan to sink a pole in the ground to hold your feeder, find a place at least ten feet from any tree or roof. A pole mounted on a stand or screwed to the base of a planter may work on your patio if there aren't trees nearby. A hanging arm may be all you need for your deck or windowframe.

The second question is, what do you want to put on the pole? A ten-pound sunflower-seed feeder, a ten-ounce hummingbird feeder, a bluebird nest box, or a suet cage? Each may require a different setup, or you may decide to use a multiple-feeder pole.

Once you've picked the feeder and decided where you want to put it, other criteria become important. Durability of a pole or hanging arm is as important as how they look to you. Galvanized steel will last longer than painted steel. Oak is likely to outlast western red cedar or pine. If screws are needed, look for galvanized steel or brass.

Several companies provide ground sockets or mounting sleeves with their poles. Instead of securing the pole in concrete, sink the socket in the concrete. Then put the pole in the socket. When you mow the lawn, just pick up the pole. If you decide to move your pole, you don't have to take the concrete with it. Fill the old socket with soil and sink a new socket.

You don't have to buy a commercial pole. You can easily make one. A plumbing supply store has half-inch, three-quarter, or one-inch (outside diameter) poles and flanges.

If you've got a metal squirrel-proof feeder, all you may need is a three-foot piece of pressure-treated 2 by 3 wood. If it's a martin house, you'll need at least a twelve-foot 4 by 4 post.

Rating the Products

Single-Feeder Poles

Looker Wooden Poles

If squirrels aren't a problem, pressure-treated wood poles are very attractive. The Looker Company manufactures 3- and 4-foot pole kits made of stained spruce or western red cedar 2 by 3s. The western cedar will last longer.

Hyde Posts

The Hyde Company manufactures two 6-foot green steel posts. The two-piece ¾-inch post holds up to five pounds; it has a metal lip to hold the Hyde green polycarbonate squirrel baffle. The three-piece 1-inch post is tapered at the top to fit the company's metal flange for mounting wooden feeders. Neither pole is galvanized. Heidi's pole showed signs of rust at the joints in a year.

Heath Pole

The Heath Company manufactures a 69-inch, 1¼-inch-thick galvanized steel pole, with a ground socket and a 6 by 4-inch plastic mounting plate. If you don't mind the steel look, this pole will hold heavy wooden feeders.

Gull Lake Poles

Gull Lake offers three galvanized steel poles. The 72-i██ thick pole comes in three pieces. The only flaw is that t██ flange at the top is only an inch or so deep, and not held secu██ with a set screw. The slightest bump and the feeder's on the ground. Gull Lake's 8-foot, three-section pole accommodates feeders up to 30 inches long and 16 inches wide.

Gull also manufactures a two-piece rustproof 53-inch pole for hummingbird feeders.

K-Feeder Poles

The K-Feeder Company manufactures two 6-foot, 1-inch-thick aluminum poles with 14-inch ground sockets. The KFP fits all the K single-tube feeders. The KCP fits the K-Carousel feeder and most wooden feeders.

Hanging Arms

What a great idea: mounting a feeder on an oak hanger right outside the kitchen window for a close-up view of birds. Unless you have squirrels. Remember, squirrels can jump four feet up and climb brick and wood siding.

Go ahead and try it. If you have a Droll Yankee feeder with a three-year warranty, you might as well take advantage of the warranty. The pole will still be there, but not so the feeder.

With that caveat, let's take a look at hanging arms.

Gull Lake Hanging Arm

Gull Lake manufactures a 40-inch galvanized-steel pole with a steel clamp to fit on decks, fences, and railings (up to 2½ inches thick). The pole itself won't rust, but the clamp, if the black enamel finish is nicked, will.

two adjustable hanging arms, 36 and
at for mounting squirrel-proof feeders
on windows and decks.

_es_

Vari-Cra...   -2) pole assembly is the most durable and versa-
tile on the mu...et today. It's made of ¾-inch galvanized conduit
pipe, corrosion-resistant hardware, die-cast connectors, plastic
mountings, and end caps. Like an Erector Set, you can set up this
pole four ways:

1. In the 80-inch mode, it fits any feeder with a ½-inch threaded base
   mount, such as a Droll Yankee or Aspects.
2. In the 88-inch mode, one feeder will hang from it.
3. In the 76-inch mode, two feeders will hang from it.
4. In the rotated 88-inch mode, any feeder regardless of length will hang
   from it.

Hyde Triple Hanger Pole

Hyde's Triple Hanger pole has three ⁵⁄₁₆-inch rustproof steel rods
inserted into its basic three-section 6-foot green pole. Be careful
inserting the three rods—the steel nipple is extremely thin. When
it stretches, and it will over time, the three rods spin together in
the wind. Insert a finishing nail between the steel rods to keep them
from slipping together.

Cardinal American Bird Feeder Station

This is our favorite pole. It looks like one of those Sears clotheslines
mom used to use. The black pole comes with four balanced hangers, a squirrel baffle, and a ground socket. Most squirrels make
easy work of the baffle. You can fortify it by slathering the under-
side with cayenne pepper and Vaseline. Replace the rubber gasket
with a metal auto-radiator hose clamp, and you're set.

10

RESOURCES FOR BACKYARD BIRDWATCHERS

Wherever you live, you're probably not too far from a store that sells backyard bird supplies: gift shops, hardware stores, feed stores, supermarkets, pet shops and garden centers, bird clubs, and wild bird specialty stores. Look in your Yellow Pages under "Birds," "Feed," or "Seed." Feeding wild birds has become so popular that you can find wild bird specialty stores in many cities. You can also buy feeders, houses, books, and food through the mail. Many general-purpose mail order companies sell bird gadgets; and there are over a dozen mail order companies that specialize in wild bird products.

Regardless of where you buy your backyard bird supplies, be skeptical of packaging information, catalog descriptions, and manufacturer's instructions. Trust your judgment, experience, (and, we hope, our recommendations). The bird-gadget industry is subject to few regulations and standards.

You're less likely to go wrong if you keep the following in mind wherever you shop:

1. Ask for a written guarantee.
2. Don't be awed by endorsements. An endorsement (actual or implied) by the National Audubon Society or other wildlife organization does not guarantee product quality.
3. Be skeptical about anecdotal advice. Everyone is happy to give advice about feeding birds. Surprisingly few birding groups, writers, retailers, and manufacturers offer scientific data to support what they say. Your best source is the U.S. Fish and Wildlife Service.
4. If you're not happy with it, take it back. If you buy a product that does not perform as advertised, return it to the manufacturer and demand an explanation.

Where to Learn More

United States

The U.S. Fish and Wildlife Service is the federal agency responsible for the conservation of migratory birds. They operate the National Wildlife Refuge system, issue bird-banding and wildlife rehabilitation permits, conduct field research, and enforce the laws that protect migratory birds.

As you get hooked on birds, you'll want to take advantage of the free publications and educational programs they offer. For more information contact the Division of National Wildlife Refuges and the Office of Migratory Bird Management, U.S. Fish and Wildlife Service, Washington, D.C. 20240.

State wildlife agencies are also a wealth of information on birds, places to see birds, and local bird clubs. For more information contact:

Director, Division of Game and Fish, Department of Conservation and Natural Resources, 64 North Union Street, Montgomery, Ala. 36193

Director, Game Division, Department of Fish and Game, P.O. Box 3-2000, Juneau, Alaska 99802

Supervisor, Non-Game Branch, Game and Fish Department, 2222 W. Greenway Road, Phoenix, Ariz. 85023

Director, Game and Fish Commission, 2 Natural Resources Drive, Little Rock, Ark. 72205

Director, Department of Fish and Game, 1416 Ninth Street, Sacramento, Calif. 95814

Director, Division of Wildlife, Department of Natural Resources, 1313 Sherman, Denver, Colo. 80203

Director, Wildlife Bureau, Department of Environmental Protection, State Office Building, 165 Capitol Avenue, Hartford, Conn. 06106

Manager, Wildlife Division, Department of Natural Resources, P.O. Box 1401, Dover, Dela. 19903

State Program Leader, Agricultural and Natural Resources, D.C. Cooperative Extension, 4200 Connecticut Avenue N.W., Washington, D.C. 20008

Director, Division of Wildlife, Game and Fresh Water Fish Commission, 620 S. Meridian Street, Tallahassee, Fla. 32301

Director, Game and Fish Division, Department of Natural Resources, Floyd Towers East, 205 Butler Street, Atlanta, Ga. 30334

Chief, Aquatic and Wildlife Resources, P.O. Box 2950, Agana, Guam 96921

Wildlife Chief, Department of Land and Natural Resources, Box 621, Honolulu, Hawaii 96809

Chief, Wildlife Division, Fish and Game Department, Box 25, Boise, Idaho 83707

Chief, Wildlife Resources Division, Department of Conservation, Lincoln Tower Plaza, 524 South Second Street, Springfield, Ill. 62706

Head, Division of Fish and Wildlife, Department of Natural Resources, 608 State Office Building, Indianapolis, Ind. 46204

Chief, Wildlife Bureau, Department of Natural Resources, East Ninth and Grand Avenue, Des Moines, Iowa 50319-0034

Director, Fish and Game Commission, Box 45A, R.R. 2, Pratt, Kans. 67124

Director, Division of Wildlife, Department of Fish and Wildlife Resources, 1 Game Farm Road, Frankfort, Ky. 40601

Chief, Division of Game, Department of Wildlife and Fisheries, P.O. Box 15570, Baton Rouge, La. 70895

Commissioner, Department of Inland Fisheries and Wildlife, 284 State Street, Station 41, Augusta, Maine 04333

Director, Forest, Park and Wildlife Service, Department of Natural Resources, Tawes State Office Building, Annapolis, Md. 21401

Director, Non-Game & Endangered Species Section, Department of Fisheries and Wildlife, 100 Cambridge Street, Boston, Mass. 02202

Chief, Wildlife Division, Department of Natural Resources, Box 30028, Lansing, Mich. 48909

Chief, Wildlife Section, Department of Natural Resources, 500 Lafayette Road, St. Paul, Minn. 55146

Director, Bureau of Fisheries and Wildlife, Department of Wildlife Conservation, P.O. Box 451, Jackson, Miss. 39205

Chief, Wildlife Division, Department of Conservation, P.O. Box 180, Jefferson City, Mo. 65102

Administrator, Wildlife Division, Department of Fish, Wildlife and Parks, 1420 East Sixth, Helena, Mont. 59620

Chief of Wildlife, Game and Parks Commission, P.O. Box 30370, Lincoln, Nebr. 68503

Director, Department of Wildlife, Box 10768, Reno, Nev. 89520

Executive Director, Fish and Game Department, 34 Bridge Street, Concord, N.H. 03301

Program Manager, Non-Game and Endangered Species, Division of Fish, Game and Wildlife, C.N. 400, Trenton, N.J. 08625

Chief, Game Management Division, Game and Fish Department, Villagra Building, Santa Fe, N.M. 87503

Chief, Bureau of Wildlife, Department of Environmental Conservation, 50 Wolf Road, Albany, N.Y. 12233

Chief, Division of Wildlife Management, Wildlife Resources Commission, 512 North Salisbury Street, Raleigh, N.C. 27611

Commissioner, Game and Fish Department, 100 North Bismark Expressway, Bismark, N.D. 58501

Chief, Division of Wildlife, Department of Natural Resources, Fountain Square, Columbus, Ohio 43224

Director, Department of Wildlife Conservation, P.O. Box 53465, Oklahoma City, Okla. 73152

Assistant Director for Wildlife, Department of Fish and Wildlife, P.O. Box 3503, Portland, Oreg. 97208

Director, Bureau of Game Management, Game Commission, P.O. Box 1567, Harrisburg, Pa. 17105-1567

Secretary, Department of Natural Resources, P.O. Box 5887, Puerta de Tierra Station, San Juan, P.R. 00906

Chief, Division of Fish and Wildlife, Department of Environmental Management, 83 Park Street, Providence, R.I. 02903

Director, Division of Conservation, Wildlife and Marine Resources Department, P.O. Box 167, Columbia, S.C. 29202

Wildlife Division Director, Game Fish and Parks Department, 445 East Capitol, Pierre, S. Dak. 57501-3185

Chief, Wildlife Management Division, Wildlife Resources Agency, P.O. Box 40747, Nashville, Tenn. 37204

Director, Wildlife Division, Parks and Wildlife Department, 4200 Smith School Road, Austin, Tex. 78744

Chief, Non-Game Management, Division of Wildlife Resources, 1596 West North Temple, Salt Lake City, Utah 84116-3154

Director of Wildlife, Department of Fish and Wildlife, 103 South Main Street, Waterbury, Vt. 05676

Director, Division of Fish and Wildlife, Department of Conservation, P.O. Box 4399, St. Thomas, V.I. 00801

Chief, Game Division, Commission of Game and Inland Fisheries, Box 11104, Richmond, Va. 23230

Chief, Wildlife Management, Department of Game, 600 North Capitol Way, Olympia, Wash. 98504

Chief of Wildlife Resources, Department of Natural Resources, 1800 Washington Street East, Charleston, W.V. 25305

Director, Bureau of Wildlife Management, Department of Natural Resources, Box 7921, Madison, Wis. 53707

Director, Game and Fish Department, Cheyenne, Wyo. 82002

Canada

Director, Canadian Wildlife Service, Ottawa, Ontario K1A 0E7

Director of Wildlife, Department of Energy and Natural Resources, 9945-108 Street, Edmonton, Alberta T5K 2C9

Wildlife Management Branch Director, Ministry of Environment, Parliament Buildings, Victoria, British Columbia V8V 1X5

Director Wildlife Branch, Department of Natural Resources, Box 24, Winnipeg, Manitoba R3H 0W9

Chief, Wildlife Management, Department of Natural Resources and Energy, P.O. Box 6000, Fredericton, New Brunswick E3B 5H1

Director, Wildlife Division, P.O. Box 4750, St. John's, Newfoundland A1C 5T7

Director, Wildlife Management, Department of Renewable Resources, Yellowknife, Northwest Territories X1A 2L9

Director of Wildlife, Department of Lands and Forests, P.O. Box 698, Halifax, Nova Scotia B3J 2T9

Director of Wildlife, Ministry of Natural Resources, Toronto, Ontario M7A 1W3

Director, Fish and Wildlife Division, P.O. Box 2000, Charlottetown, Prince Edward Island C1A 7N8

Director, Fish and Game, Place de la Capitale, 150 East St. Cyrille Boulevard, Quebec City, Quebec G1R 2B2

Wildlife Director, Department of Parks and Renewable Resources, 3211 Albert Street, Regina, Saskatchewan S4S 5W6

Director, Fish and Wildlife, Department of Renewable Resources, Box 2703, Whitehorse, Yukon Territory Y1A 2C6

Bird Clubs

Regardless of where you live, there's a bird club nearby. We encourage you to join them. It's a great way to meet people who share your interest in birds and to learn more about birds. Take advantage of their many field trips, lectures, and publications.

United States

Birmingham Audubon Society, P.O. Box 314, Birmingham, Ala. 35201

Anchorage Audubon Society, P.O. Box 1161, Anchorage, Alaska 99510
Fairbanks Bird Club, P.O. Box 81791, Fairbanks, Alaska 99708

Northern Arizona Audubon Society, P.O. Box 1496, Sedona, Ariz. 86336
Tucson Audubon Society, P.O. Box 3981, Tucson, Ariz. 85717

Arkansas Audubon Society, Museum of Science and Natural History, MacArthur Park, Little Rock, Ark. 72202

Golden Gate Audubon Society, 2718 Telegraph Avenue, Berkeley, Calif. 94705
Los Angeles Audubon Society, 7377 Santa Monica Boulevard, Los Angeles, Calif. 90046
Morro Coast Audubon Society, P.O. Box 160, Morro Bay, Calif. 93442
Mt. Shasta Area Audubon Society, Box 530, Mt. Shasta, Calif. 96067
Point Reyes Bird Observatory, 4990 State Route One, Stinson Beach, Calif. 94970
San Diego Audubon Society, 4536 Park Boulevard, San Diego, Calif. 92116
San Francisco Bay Bird Observatory, Box 247, Alviso, Calif. 95002
Santa Barbara Audubon Society, c/o Santa Barbara Museum of Natural History, 2559 Puerta del Sol Road, Santa Barbara, Calif. 93105

Boulder Audubon Society, P.O. Box 2081, Boulder, Colo. 80306
Denver Field Ornithologists, Denver Museum of Natural History, City Park, Denver, Colo. 80205

Connecticut Ornithological Association, 314 Unquowa Road, Fairfield, Conn. 06530
New Haven Bird Club, Peabody Museum, Yale University, Whitney and Sachem, New Haven, Conn. 06520

Delmarva Ornithological Society, P.O. Box 4247, Greenville, Del. 19807

Florida Audubon Society, 1101 Audubon Way, Maitland, Fla. 32751

Georgia Ornithological Society, P.O. Box 38214, Atlanta, Ga. 30334

Hawaii Audubon Society, P.O. Box 22832, Honolulu, Hawaii 96822

Idaho Ornithological Council, Biology Department, Idaho State University, Pocatell, Idaho 83201

Chicago Ornithological Society, Field Museum of Natural History, Roosevelt Road at Lake Shore Drive, Chicago, Ill. 60605
Illinois Audubon Society, P.O. Box 608, Wayne, Ill. 60184
North Central Illinois Ornithological Society, Burpee Museum of Natural History, 813 North Main Street, Rockford, Ill. 61103
Ornithology Section, Peoria Academy of Science, P.O. Box 3094, Peoria, Ill. 61614

Indiana Audubon Society, Mary Gray Bird Sanctuary, Box 163, Connersville, Ind. 47331

Iowa Ornithologists Union, 825 7th Avenue, Iowa City, Iowa 52240

Kansas Ornithological Society, 18 Circle Drive, Newton, Kans. 67114

Kentucky Ornithological Society, Biology Department, University of Louisville, Louisville, Ky. 40208

Louisiana Ornithological Society, Museum of Natural Science, Louisiana State University, Baton Rouge, La. 70803

Maine Audubon Society, 118 Route One, Falmouth, Maine 04105

Maryland Ornithological Society, Cylburn Mansion, 4915 Greenspring Avenue, Baltimore, Md. 21209

Cape Cod Bird Club, Cape Cod Museum of Natural History, Route 6-A, Brewster, Mass. 02631
Manomet Bird Observatory, Box 936, Manomet, Mass. 02345
Nuttall Ornithological Club, Museum of Comparative Zoology, Harvard University, Cambridge, Mass. 02351

Michigan Audubon Society, 409 West E Avenue, Kalamazoo, Mich. 49007

Minnesota Ornithologists' Union, Bell Museum of Natural History, 10 Church Street, S.E., Minneapolis, Minn. 55455

Mississippi Ornithological Society, Museum of Natural Science, 111 North Jefferson, Jackson, Miss. 39202

Audubon Society of Missouri, 3906 Grace Ellen Drive, Columbia, Mo. 65202-1796

Five Valleys Audubon Society, P.O. Box 8425, Missoula, Mont. 59801

Nebraska Ornithologists Union, University of Nebraska State Museum, Lincoln, Nebr. 68508

Lahontan Audubon Society, P.O. Box 2304, Reno, Nev. 89505
Red Rock Audubon Society, P.O. Box 42944, Las Vegas, Nev. 89104

Audubon Society of New Hampshire, P.O. Box 528 B, Concord, N.H. 03302-0516

Urner Ornithological Club, Newark Museum, 43-49 Washington Street, Newark, N.J. 07101

New Mexico Ornithological Society, Biology Department, New Mexico State University, Las Cruces, N. Mex. 88003

Audubon Society of New York, 8 Wade Road, Latham, N.Y. 12110
Buffalo Ornithological Society, Buffalo Museum of Science, Humbolt Park, Buffalo, N.Y. 14211
Federation of New York State Bird Clubs, P.O. Box 362, Mt. Kisco, N.Y. 10549-0362
Linnaean Society of New York, American Museum of Natural History, Central Park West at 79th Street, New York, N.Y. 10024

Carolina Bird Club, P.O. Box 27647, Raleigh, N.C. 27611

North Dakota Natural Science Society, P.O. Box 8238, University Station, Grand Forks, N. Dak. 58202-8238

Cincinnati Bird Club, Cincinnati Nature Center, 4949 Tealtown Road, Milford, Ohio 45150
Dayton Audubon Society, Dayton Museum of Natural History, 2629 Ridge Avenue, Dayton, Ohio 45414
Ohio Audubon Council, 3776 Wales Avenue N.W., Massillon, Ohio 44646

Oklahoma Ornithological Society, Route 7, Box 62, Tahlequah, Okla. 74464

Portland Audubon Society, 5151 Northwest Cornell Road, Portland, Oreg. 97210

Audubon Society of Western Pennsylvania, 614 Dorseyville Road, Pittsburgh, Pa. 15238
Delaware Valley Ornithological Club, Academy of Natural Sciences, 19th and The Parkway, Philadelphia, Pa. 19103

Natural History Society of Puerto Rico, G.P.O. Box 1036, San Juan, P.R. 00919

Audubon Society of Rhode Island, 12 Sanderson Road, Smithfield, R.I. 02917

Charleston Natural History Society, P.O. Box 504, Charleston, S.C. 29404

South Dakota Ornithologists Union, 3220 Kirkwood Drive, Rapid City, S. Dak. 57702

Tennessee Ornithological Society, P.O. Box 402, Norris, Tenn. 37828

Dallas County Audubon Society, 723 Kirkwood Drive, Dallas, Tex. 75218
Houston Outdoor Nature Club, 4141 South Braeswood, Box 101, Houston, Tex. 77025
Texas Ornithological Society, 326 Live Oak, Ingram, Tex. 78025
Travis Audubon Society, 1807 A Blue Crest, Austin, Tex. 78704

Utah Nature Study Society, 1144 East Third South, Salt Lake City, Utah 84102

Vermont Institute of Natural Science, Church Hill Road, Woodstock, Vt. 05091

Virginia Society of Ornithology, 520 Rainbow Forest Drive, Lynchburg, Va. 24502

Seattle Audubon Society, Fourth Avenue and Pike Street, Seattle, Wash. 98101

Brooks Bird Club, 707 Warwood Avenue, Wheeling, W. Va. 26003

Wisconsin Society for Ornithology, 6917 North Highway 83, Hartland, Wis. 53029

Alpine Audubon Society, 710½ Ivinson Avenue, Laramie, Wyo. 82070

Canada

Federation of Alberta Naturalists, Box 1472, Edmonton, Alberta T5J 2N5

Federation of British Columbia Naturalists, 1200 Hornby Street, Vancouver, British Columbia V6Z 2E2

Manitoba Naturalists Society, 1770 Notre Dame Avenue, Winnipeg, Manitoba R3E 3K2

New Brunswick Federation of Naturalists, New Brunswick Museum, 277 Douglas Avenue, St. John, New Brunswick E2K 1E5

Newfoundland Natural History Society, P.O. Box 1013, St. John's, Newfoundland A1C 5M3

Nova Scotia Bird Society, Nova Scotia Museum, 1747 Summer Street, Halifax, Nova Scotia B3H 3A6

Federation of Ontario Naturalists, 1262 Don Mills Road, Don Mills, Ontario M3B 2W7

Natural History Society of Prince Edward Island, P.O. Box 2346, Charlottetown, Prince Edward Island C1A 7NB

Society for the Protection of Birds, 4832 de Maisonneuve Boulevard West, Montreal, Quebec H3Z 1M5

Club Des Ornithologues Du Quebec, Jardin Zoo, 8191 de Zoo, Orsainville, Quebec G1G 4G4

Saskatchewan Natural History Society, P.O. Box 1784, Saskatoon, Saskatchewan S7K 3S1

Yukon Conservation Society, P.O. Box 4163, Whitehorse, Yukon Territory Y1A 2C6

Periodicals

American Birds, National Audubon Society, 950 Third Avenue, New York, N.Y. 10022

Birding, American Birding Association, P.O. Box 6599, Colorado Springs, Colo. 80934

Bird Watch, Bird Populations Institute, Box 637, Manhattan, Kans. 66502

Bird Watcher's Digest, Box 110, Marietta, Ohio 45750

Birder's World, 720 East 8 Street, Holland, Mich. 49423

Dick E. Bird News, P.O. Box 377, Acme, Mich. 49601

Living Bird Quarterly, Laboratory or Ornithology, Cornell University, 159 Sapsucker Woods Road, Ithaca, N.Y. 14850

Natural History, American Museum of Natural History, Central Park West at 79th Street, New York, N.Y. 10024

Nature Canada, 75 Albert Street, Ottawa, Ontario, Canada K1P 6GI

Wild Bird Observer, American Wild Bird Company, 802 Cabin John Parkway, Rockville, Md. 20852

WildBird, Box 57900, Los Angeles, Calif. 90057

APPENDIX: BIRD BOOKS AND TAPES

Some of the following books are out of print, but are included because of their lasting value. Readers can find them in university libraries or used bookstores.

Attracting Birds

Cerulean, L.; C. Botha; and D. Legare. 1986. *Planting a refuge for wildlife: How to create a backyard habitat for Florida's birds and beasts.* Tallahassee: Florida Game and Freshwater Fish Commission.

DeGraaf, Richard, and G. M. Whitman. 1979. *Trees, shrubs and vines for attracting wildlife.* Amherst: University of Massachusetts Press.

Harrison, Kit and George. 1983. *America's favorite backyard birds.* New York: Simon and Schuster.

Henderson, Carrol. 1987. *Landscaping for wildlife.* Minneapolis: Minnesota Department of Natural Resources.

Hughes, Heidi, 1989. *Backyard bird feeding.* Washington, D.C.: U.S. Fish & Wildlife Service.

Layton, R. B. 1983. *Birds that will build in bird houses.* Jackson, Miss.: Nature Books Publishers.

Martin, A. C.; H. S. Zim; and A. L. Nelson. 1961. *American wildlife and plants: A guide to wildlife food habits.* New York: Dover.

Field Identification Guides

Farrand, John, ed. 1983. *Audubon master guide to birding.* New York: Knopf.

Harrison, Colin. 1984. *A field guide to the nests, eggs and nestlings of North American birds.* Lexington, Mass.: Stephen Greene.

Harrison, Hal. 1975. *Field guide to eastern birds' nests.* Boston: Houghton Mifflin.

———. 1979. *Field guide to western birds' nests.* Boston: Houghton Mifflin.

Headstrom, Richard. 1961. *Birds' nests: A field guide.* New York: Ives Washburn.

National Geographic Society. 1987. *Field guide to the birds of North America.* Washington, D.C.: National Geographic Society.

Peterson, Roger T. 1980. *Field guide to birds of eastern and central North America.* Boston: Houghton Mifflin.

———. 1961. *Field guide to western birds.* Boston: Houghton Mifflin.

Robbins, C.; B. Bruun; and H. Zim. 1983. *Birds of North America.* New York: Western Publishing.

Stallcup, Rich. 1985. *Birds for real.* Inverness, Calif.: Stallcup.

Bird Songs

Borror, Donald. *Common bird songs.* New York: Dover Publications.

———. *Songs of eastern birds.* New York: Dover Publications.

———. *Songs of western birds.* New York: Dover Publications.

———. *Florida bird songs.* New York: Dover Publications.

———. *Bird song and bird behavior.* New York: Dover Publications.

Borror, Donald, and William Gunn. 1985. *Warblers of North America.* Ithaca: Cornell Laboratory of Ornithology.

Jellis, Rosemary. 1984. *Bird sounds and their meaning.* Ithaca: Cornell University Press.

Walton, Richard, and R. Lawson. 1989. *Birding by ear.* Boston: Houghton Mifflin.

Life Histories

Blackbirds

Bent, Arthur Cleveland. 1958. *Life histories of North American blackbirds, orioles, tanagers, and allies.* Washington, D.C.: Government Printing Office.

Nero, Robert. 1983. *Redwings.* Washington, D.C.: Smithsonian Institution Press.

Orians, Gordon. 1985. *Blackbirds of the Americas.* Seattle: University of Washington Press.

Warblers

Bent, Arthur Cleveland. 1953. *Life histories of North American wood warblers.* Washington, D.C.: Government Printing Office.

Chapman, Frank. 1907. *The warblers of North America.* New York: Appleton and Company.

Griscom, Ludlow, and Alexander Sprunt. 1957. *Warblers of America*. New York: Devin-Adair.

Harrison, Hal. 1984. *Wood warblers' world*. New York: Simon & Schuster.

Meanley, Brooke. 1971. *Natural history of the Swainson's warbler*. Washington, D.C.: United States Department of the Interior.

Morse, D. H. 1989. *American warblers: An ecological and behavioral perspective*. Cambridge: Harvard University Press.

Mockingbirds

Bent, Arthur Cleveland. 1948. *Life histories of North American nuthatches, wrens, thrashers and their allies*. Washington, D.C.: Government Printing Office.

Doughty, Robin. 1988. *The mockingbird*. Austin: University of Texas Press.

Tanagers

Bent, Arthur Cleveland. 1958. *Life histories of North American blackbirds, orioles, tanagers and allies*. Washington, D.C.: Government Printing Office.

Isler, Morton, and Phyllis Isler. 1987. *The tanagers: Natural history, distribution and identification*. Washington, D.C.: Smithsonian Institution Press.

Skutch, Alexander. 1989. *Life of the tanager*. Ithaca: Cornell University Press.

Woodpeckers

Bent, Arthur Cleveland. 1939. *Life histories of North American woodpeckers*. Washington, D.C.: Government Printing Office.

Ekstrom, Fannie. 1901. *The woodpeckers*. Boston: Houghton Mifflin.

Skutch, Alexander. 1985. *Life of the woodpecker*. Ithaca: Cornell University Press.

Bluebirds

Bent, Arthur Cleveland. 1949. *Life histories of North American thrushes, kinglets and their allies*. Washington, D.C.: Government Printing Office.

Layton, R. B. 1986. *Bluebirds: Their daily lives and how to attract and raise bluebirds*. Jackson, Miss.: Nature Books Publishers.

Zeleny, Lawrence. 1974. *The bluebird: How you can help its fight for survival*. Bloomington: Indiana University Press.

Purple Martins

Allen, Robert, and Margaret Nice. 1952. *A study of the breeding biology of the purple martin*. Notre Dame, Ind.: University of Notre Dame Press.

Bent, Arthur Cleveland. 1942. *Life histories of North American flycatchers, larks swallows and their allies*. Washington, D.C.: Government Printing Office.

Layton, R. B. 1969. *The purple martin*. Jackson, Miss.: Nature Books Publishers.

Crows

Bent, Arthur Cleveland. 1946. *Life histories of North American jays, crows and titmice*. Washington, D.C.: Government Printing Office.

Goodwin, Derek. 1986. *Crows of the world*. Seattle: University of Washington Press.

Kilham, Lawrence. 1989. *The American crow and the common raven*. College Station: Texas A & M University.

Hummingbirds

Bent, Arthur Cleveland. 1940. *Life histories of North American cuckoos, goat-suckers, hummingbirds and their allies*. Washington, D.C.: Government Printing Office.

Grant, K. A., and V. Grant. 1968. *Hummingbirds and their flowers*. New York: Columbia University Press.

Greenwalt, Crawford. 1960. *Hummingbirds*. New York: Doubleday.

Johnsgard, Paul. 1983. *Hummingbirds of North America*. Washington, D.C.: Smithsonian Institution Press.

Skutch, Alexander. 1973. *The life of the hummingbird*. New York: Crown.

Tyrell, Esther, and Robert Tyrell. 1985. *Hummingbirds: Their life and behavior*. New York: Crown.

Sparrows

Bent, Arthur Cleveland. 1968. *Life histories of North American cardinals, grosbeaks, buntings, towhees, finches, sparrows and their allies*. Washington, D.C.: Government Printing Office.

Nice, Margaret. 1964. *Studies in the life history of the song sparrow*. New York: Dover.

Summers-Smith, Dennis. 1988. *The sparrows*. Vermillion, S. Dak.: Buteo Books.

Owls

Bent, Arthur Cleveland. 1938. *Life histories of North American birds of prey, part II*. Washington, D.C.: Government Printing Office.

Cameron, Angus, and Peter Parnell. 1971. *The nightwatchers.* New York: Four Winds Press.

Craighead, John, and Frank Craighead. 1970. *Hawks, owls and wildlife.* New York: Dover.

Eckert, Allan, 1974. *The owls of North America.* New York: Doubleday.

Johnsgard, Paul. 1988. *North American owls.* Washington, D.C.: Smithsonian Institution Press.

Maslow, Jonathan. 1983. *The owl papers.* New York: E. P. Dutton.

Walker, Lewis. 1974. *The book of owls.* New York: Alfred Knopf.

Hawks

Austing, Ron. 1964. *The world of the red-tailed hawk.* Philadelphia: Lippincott.

Bent, Arthur Cleveland. 1937. *Life histories of North American birds of prey, part I.* Washington, D.C.: Government Printing Office.

Brown, Leslie. 1976. *Birds of prey: Their biology and ecology.* New York: A & W Publishers.

———. 1970. *Eagles.* New York: Arco.

Clark, William, and Brian Wheeler. 1987. *Field guide to the hawks of North America.* Boston: Houghton Mifflin.

Craighead, John, and Frank Craighead. 1956. *Hawks, owls and wildlife.* New York: Dover.

Hammerstrom, Fran. 1972. *Birds of prey of Wisconsin.* Madison: Wisconsin Department of Natural Resources.

Heintzelman, Donald. 1979. *The hawks and owls of North America.* New York: Universe Books.

———. 1986. *The migration of hawks.* Bloomington: Indiana University Press.

Ratcliffe, Derek. 1980. *The peregrine falcon.* Vermillion, S. Dak.: Buteo Books.

Reference Books

Collias, N. E., and E. C. Collias. 1984. *Nest building and bird behavior.* Princeton: Princeton University Press.

Erlich, P.; D. Dobkin; and D. Wheye. 1988. *The birder's handbook.* New York: Simon and Schuster.

Leahy, Christopher. 1984. *The birdwatcher's companion: An encyclopedic handbook of North American birdlife.* New York: Bonanza.

Mead, Christopher. 1983. *Bird migration.* New York: Facts on File.

Palmer, Ralph. *Handbook of North American birds.* New Haven: Yale University Press.

1962. Loons through Flamingos.

1976. Waterfowl Parts 1 & 2.

1988. Diurnal Raptors Parts 1 & 2.

Perrins, Christopher. 1985. *The encyclopedia of birds.* New York: Facts on File.

Sutton, George, 1986. *Birds worth watching.* Norman: University of Oklahoma Press.

Biographical

Gibbons, Felton, and Deborah Strom. 1988. *Neighbors to the birds.* New York: Norton.

Kastner, Joseph. 1986. *A world of watchers.* New York: Knopf.

Nice, Margaret. 1939. *The watcher at the nest.* New York: Macmillan.

Strom, Deborah. 1986. *Birdwatching with American women.* New York: W. W. Norton.

Ornithology

Pasquier, Roger. 1977. *Watching birds.* Boston: Houghton Mifflin.

Pettingtill, Olin S. 1958. *Ornithology in laboratory and field.* Minneapolis: Burgess Publishing Co.

Welty, Joel Carl. 1982. *Life of birds.* Philadelphia: Saunders.

Squirrels

Adler, Bill, Jr. 1988. *Outwitting squirrels: 101 cunning stratagems to reduce dramatically the egregious misappropriation of seed from your birdfeeder by squirrels.* Chicago: Chicago Review Press.

Gurnell, John. 1988. *The natural history of squirrels.* New York: Facts on File.

Regional Bird Guides

Alaska

Armstrong, Robert. 1983. *New, expanded guide to the birds of Alaska.* Anchorage: Alaska Northwest.

Gabrielson, Ira, and F. C. Lincoln. 1959. *Birds of Alaska.* Philadelphia: Stackpole.

Alabama

Howell, A. H. 1928. *Birds of Alabama.* Birmingham: Department of Game and Fisheries.

Imhoff, Thomas. 1976. *Alabama birds*. University: University of Alabama Press.

Arizona

Davis, William, and Stephen Russell. 1979. *Birds in southeastern Arizona*. Tucson: Tucson Audubon Society.

Lane, James. 1988. *A birder's guide to southeastern Arizona*. Denver: L & P Press.

Monson, Gale, and Allan Phillips. 1981. *Annotated checklist of the birds of Arizona*. Tucson: University of Arizona Press.

Phillips, Allan, Joe Marshall, and Gale Monson. 1964. *The birds of Arizona*. Tucson: University of Arizona Press.

California

Dawson, William. 1923. *Birds of California*. San Diego: South Moulton.

Garrett, Kimball, and John Dunn. 1981. *Birds of southern California: Status and distribution*. Los Angeles: Los Angeles Audubon Society.

Lane, James. 1985. *A birder's guide to southern California*. Denver: L & P Press.

McCaskie, Guy, Paul DeBenedictis, Richard Erickson, and Joseph Morlan. 1979. *Birds of northern California: An annotated field checklist*. Berkeley: Golden Gate Audubon Society.

Richmond, Jean. 1985. *Birding northern California*. Walnut Creek: Mt. Diablo Audubon Society.

Roberson, Don. 1978. *Birders' California*. Colorado Springs: American Birding Association.

———. 1985. *Monterey birds*. Carmel: Monterey Peninsula Audubon Society.

Santa Barbara Museum of Natural History. 1967. *Birds of the Santa Barbara region*. Santa Barbara: Museum of Natural History.

Santa Clara Valley Audubon Society. 1983. *Birding at the bottom of the bay*. Palo Alto: Santa Clara Valley Audubon Society.

Sequoia Audubon Society. 1985. *San Francisco peninsula birdwatching*. Burlingame: Sequoia Audubon Society.

Small, Arnold. 1974. *Birds of California*. New York: Winchester Press.

Yocum, Charles, and Stanley Harris. 1975. *Birds of northwestern California*. Arcata: Humboldt State University.

Colorado

Bailey, Alfred, and Robert Niedrach. 1965. *Birds of Colorado*. Denver: Museum of Natural History.

Folzenlogen, Robert. 1986. *Birding guide to Denver-Boulder region*. Boulder: Pruett.

Johnsgard, Paul. 1986. *Birds of the Rocky Mountains*. Boulder: Colorado Association of University Presses.

Lane, James, and Harold R. Holt. 1975. *Birder's guide to eastern Colorado*. Denver: L & P Press.

Connecticut

Sage, John, Louis Bishop, and Walter Bliss. 1913. *The birds of Connecticut*. Hartford: State of Connecticut Geological and Natural History Survey.

Walton, Richard. 1988. *Bird finding in New England*. Boston: Godine.

Delaware

Delmarva Ornithological Society. 1978. *Where to look for birds on the Delmarva Peninsula*. Greenville, Del.: Delmarva Ornithological Society.

Harding, John, and Justin Harding. 1980. *Birding the Delaware Valley region: A comprehensive guide to birdwatching in southeastern Pennsylvania, central and southern New Jersey and northcentral Delaware*. Philadelphia: Temple University Press.

District of Columbia

Briggs, Shirley, and Chandler Robbins. 1951. *Where birds live: Habitats in the Middle Atlantic states*. Washington, D.C.: Audubon Society of the District of Columbia.

Stewart, Robert, and Chandler Robbins. 1958. *Birds of Maryland and the District of Columbia*. Washington, D.C.: U.S. Department of the Interior.

Wilds, Claudia. 1983. *Finding birds in the national capital area*. Washington, D.C.: Smithsonian Institution Press.

Florida

Bailey, Harold. 1925. *Birds of Florida*. Tallahassee: Williams and Wilkins Company.

Florida Audubon Society. 1979. *Where to find birds in Florida*. Maitland: Florida Audubon Society.

Hall, Francis. 1979. *Birds of Florida*. St. Petersburg: Great Outdoors Publishing Company.

Hewitt, Oliver. 1976. *Field book of birds of the Florida suncoast*. Sarasota: Mote Marine Laboratory.

Howell, Arthur A. 1932. *Florida bird life*. Tallahassee: Florida Department of Game and Freshwater Fish.

Lane, James. *Birder's guide to Florida*. 1984. Denver: L & P Press.

Sprunt, Alexander. 1954. *Florida bird life*. New York: Coward-McCann.

Tall Timbers Research Station. 1965. *A survey of birdlife of northwestern Florida*. Tallahassee: Tall Timbers Research Station.

Tampa Audubon Society. 1978. *Where to find birds in the Tampa Bay area*. Tampa: Tampa Audubon Society.

Tucker, James. 1968. *Florida birds: How to attract, feed and know them*. Tampa: Lewis Maxwell Publisher.

Bond, James. 1980. *Birds of the West Indies*. Boston: Houghton Mifflin.

Georgia

Burleigh, Thomas. 1958. *Georgia birds*. Norman: University of Oklahoma Press.

Hawaii

Berger, Andrew. 1981. *Hawaiian birdlife*. Honolulu: University of Hawaii Press.

Pratte, Douglas, Phillip Bruner, and Delwyn Berrett. 1987. *A field guide to the birds of Hawaii and the tropical Pacific*. Princeton: Princeton University Press.

Pyle, Robert. 1988. *A checklist of the birds of Hawaii*. Honolulu: Hawaii Audubon Society.

Shallenberger, Robert. 1978. *Hawaii's birds*. Honolulu: Hawaii Audubon Society.

Illinois

Bohlen, H. David. 1989. *The birds of Illinois*. Bloomington: Indiana University Press.

Fawks, Elton, and Paul Lobik. 1975. *Bird-finding in Illinois*. Downers Grove: Illinois Audubon Society.

Indiana

Brock, Kenneth. 1986. *Birds of the Indiana Dunes*. Bloomington: Indiana University Press.

Keller, Charles E.; S. A. Keller; and T. C. Keller. 1986. *Indiana birds and their haunts*. Bloomington: Indiana University Press.

Iowa

Dinsmore, James, et al. 1983. *Iowa birds*. Ames: Iowa State University Press.

Kansas

Goodrich, Arthur. 1945. *Birds in Kansas.* Topeka: State Printer.

Johnson, Richard. 1964. *Breeding birds in Kansas.* Lawrence: University of Kansas Press.

Thompson, M. C., and Ely. 1989. *Birds in Kansas.* Lawrence: University of Kansas Press.

Zimmerman, John, and Sebastian Patti. 1988. *A guide to bird finding in Kansas and western Missouri.* Lawrence: University Press of Kansas.

Kentucky

Barbour, Roger, Clell Peterson, Delbert Rust, Herbert Shadowen, and A. L. Whitt. 1973. *Kentucky birds: A finding guide.* Lexington: University of Kentucky Press.

Louisiana

Lowrey, George. 1974. *Louisiana birds.* Baton Rouge: Louisiana State University Press.

Oberholser, Harry. 1938. *Bird life of Louisiana.* New Orleans: Department of Conservation.

Maine

Palmer, Ralph. 1949. *Maine birds.* Cambridge: Museum of Comparative Zoology.

Pettingill, Olin, Richard Anderson, and Irving Richardson. 1976. *Enjoying Maine birds.* Portland: Maine Audubon Society.

Pierson, Elizabeth, and Jan Pierson. 1981. *Birder's guide to the coast of Maine.* Camden, Maine: Down East.

Maryland

Briggs, Shirley, and Chandler Robbins. 1951. *Where birds live: Habitats in the middle Atlantic states.* Washington, D.C.: Audubon Society of the District of Columbia.

Stewart, Robert, and Chandler Robbins. 1958. *Birds of Maryland and the District of Columbia.* Washington, D.C.: U.S. Department of the Interior.

Wilds, Claudia. 1983. *Finding birds in the national capital area.* Washington, D.C.: Smithsonian Institution Press.

Massachusetts

Bagg, A. C., and S. A. Eliot. 1937. *Birds of the Connecticut Valley in Massachusetts*. North Hampton: Hampshire Bookshop.

Forbush, Edward. 1925–29. *Birds of Massachusetts and other New England states*. 3 vols. Norwood: Massachusetts Department of Agriculture.

Griscom, Ludlow. 1949. *Birds of Concord*. Cambridge: Harvard University Press.

Griscom, Ludlow, and Guy Emerson. 1959. *Birds of Martha's Vineyard*. Portland: Anthoesen Press.

Griscom, Ludlow, and E. Floger. 1948. *Birds of Nantucket*. Cambridge: Harvard University Press.

Griscom, Ludlow, and Dorothy Snyder. 1955. *Birds of Massachusetts*. Salem: Peabody Museum.

Hill, Norman. 1965. *Birds of Cape Cod*. New York: William Morrow and Company.

Leahy, Christopher. 1975. *An introduction to Massachusetts birds*. Lincoln: Massachusetts Audubon Society.

Walton, Richard. 1988. *Bird finding in New England*. Boston: Godine.

Michigan

Barrows, Walter. 1912. *Michigan bird life*. Lansing: Michigan Agricultural College.

Wood, Norman. 1951. *Birds of Michigan*. Ann Arbor: University of Michigan Press.

Minnesota

Eckert, Kim. 1983. *A birder's guide to Minnesota*. Minneapolis: Minnesota Ornithologists Union.

Green, Janet, and Robert Janssen. 1975. *Minnesota birds: Where, when and how many*. Minneapolis: University of Minnesota Press.

Janssen, Robert. 1987. *Birds in Minnesota*. Minneapolis: University of Minnesota.

Mississippi

Burleigh, T. D. 1944. *Bird life of the gulf coast region of Mississippi*. Baton Rouge: Louisiana State University Museum of Zoology.

Troups, Judith, and Jerome Jackson. 1987. *Birds and birding on the Mississippi coast*. Jackson: University Press of Mississippi.

Missouri

Zimmerman, John, and Sebastian Patti. 1988. *A guide to bird finding in Kansas and western Missouri*. Lawrence: University Press of Kansas.

Montana

Ulrich, Tom. 1984. *Birds of the northern Rockies*. Missoula: Mountain Press Publishing Company.

Nebraska

Johnsgard, Paul. 1979. *Birds of the Great Plains*. Lincoln: University of Nebraska Press.

New Hampshire

Elkins, Kimball. 1982. *Checklist of the birds of New Hampshire*. Concord: New Hampshire Audubon Society.

Ridgely, Beverly. 1987. *Birds of the Squam Lakes region*. Plymouth: Squam Lakes Association.

Walton, Richard. 1988. *Bird finding in New England*. Boston: Godine.

New Jersey

Boyle, William. 1986. *A guide to bird finding in New Jersey*. New Brunswick: Rutgers University Press.

Harding, John, and Justin Harding. 1980. *Birding the Delaware Valley region: A comprehensive guide to birdwatching in southeastern Pennsylvania, central and southern New Jersey and northcentral Delaware*. Philadelphia: Temple University Press.

Leck, Charles. 1975. *Birds of New Jersey: Their habits and habitats*. New Brunswick: Rutgers University Press.

————. 1984. *The status and distribution of New Jersey's birds*. New Brunswick: Rutgers University Press.

Stone, Witmer. 1965. *Bird studies at Old Cape May*. New York: Dover.

New York

Bull, John. 1985. *Birds of New York State*. Ithaca: Cornell University Press.

———. 1964. *Birds of the New York area.* New York: Harper and Row.

Drennan, Susan. 1981. *Where to find birds in New York State.* Syracuse: Syracuse University Press.

North Carolina

Pearson, T. G.; C. S. Brimley; and H. H. Brimley. 1942. *The birds of North Carolina.* North Carolina Department of Agriculture.

Potter, Eloise, J. F. Parnell, and R. P. Teulings. *Birds of the Carolinas.* Chapel Hill: University of North Carolina Press.

North Dakota

Lane, James, and Kevin Zimmer. 1979. *Birder's guide to North Dakota.* Denver: L & P Press.

Ohio

Cincinnati Nature Center. 1978. *Birds of the Cincinnati area.* Cincinnati: Nature Center.

Dawson, William. 1902. *The birds of Ohio.* Columbus: Wheaton Publishing Company.

Peterjohn, Bruce. 1989. *The birds of Ohio.* Bloomington: Indiana University Press.

Thompson, Tom. 1983. *Birding in Ohio.* Bloomington: Indiana University Press.

Oklahoma

Sutton, George. 1967. *Oklahoma birds: Their ecology and distribution with comments on the avifauna of the southern Great Plains.* Norman: University of Oklahoma Press.

———. 1987. *Fifty common birds of Oklahoma and the southern Great Plains.* Norman: University of Oklahoma Press.

Tulsa Audubon Society. 1986. *Guide to birding in Oklahoma.* Tulsa: Tulsa Audubon Society.

———. 1988. *Birds of Tulsa County.* Tulsa: Tulsa Audubon Society.

Oregon

Farner, Donald. 1952. *Birds of Crater Lake National Park.* Lawrence: University of Kansas Press.

Pennsylvania

Harding, John, and Justin Harding. 1980. *Birding the Delaware Valley region: A comprehensive guide to birdwatching in southeastern Pennsylvania, central and southern New Jersey and northcentral Delaware.* Philadelphia: Temple University Press.

Todd, W. E. 1940. *Birds of western Pennsylvania.* Pittsburgh: University of Pittsburgh Press.

Warren, B. H. 1890. *Birds of Pennsylvania.* Harrisburg: State Printer.

Wood, M. 1973. *Birds of Pennsylvania: When and where to find them.* University Park: Pennsylvania State University.

Rhode Island

Rhode Island Ornithological Club. 1983. *Checklist of Rhode Island birds.* Providence: Rhode Island Ornithological Club.

South Carolina

Hilton Head Island Audubon Society. 1988. *Birder's guide to Hilton Head and Low Country.* Hilton Head: Hilton Head Island Audubon Society.

Potter, Eloise, James Parnell, and Robert Teulings. 1980. *Birds of the Carolinas.* Chapel Hill: University of North Carolina Press.

Sprunt, Alexander, and E. B. Chamberlain. 1970. *South Carolina bird life.* Columbia: University of South Carolina Press.

Tennessee

Bierly, Michael. 1980. *Birdfinding in Tennessee.* Nashville: Bierly.

Texas

Arnold, Keith. 1984. *Checklist of birds of Texas.* Austin: Texas Ornithological Society.

Kutac, Edward. 1982. *Texas birds: Where they are and how to find them.* Houston: Gulf Publishing Company.

Kutac, Edward, and Christopher Caran. 1976. *A bird finding and naturalist's guide for the Austin, Texas area.* Austin: Austin Natural Science Association.

Lane, James, and Harold R. Holt. 1986. *Birder's guide to the Rio Grande Valley.* Denver: L & P Press.

Lane, James, John Tveten, and Harold R. Holt. 1984. *Birder's guide to the Texas coast.* Denver: L & P Press.

Oberholser, Harry, and Edgar Kincaid. 1974. *The bird life of Texas.* Austin: University of Texas Press.

Peterson, Roger T. 1963. *A field guide to the birds of Texas and adjacent states.* Boston: Houghton Mifflin.

Pulich, Warren. 1988. *Birds of north central Texas.* College Station: Texas A & M University Press.

Rappole, John, and Gene Blacklock. 1985. *Birds of the Texas coastal bend.* College Station: Texas A & M University.

Rockport-Fulton Chamber of Commerce and Audubon Outdoor Club of Corpus Christi. 1989. *Birder's guide to Rockport-Fulton.*

Wauer, Roland. 1973. *Birds of Big Bend National Park and vicinity.* Austin: University of Texas Press.

———. 1985. *Field guide to the birds of the Big Bend.* Austin: Texas Monthly Press.

Utah

Behle, William. 1958. *Bird life of the Great Salt Lake.* Salt Lake City: University of Utah Press.

Behle, William, and Michael Perry. 1975. *Utah birds: Guide, checklist and occurrence charts.* Salt Lake City: Utah Museum of Natural History.

Hayward, Lynn, et al. 1976. *Birds of Utah.* Salt Lake City: Brigham Young University Press.

Wauer, Roland, and Dennis Carter. 1965. *Birds of Zion National Park and vicinity.* Springdale, Utah: Zion Natural History Association.

Vermont

Ellison, W. G. 1981. *A guide to bird-finding in Vermont.* Woodstock: Vermont Institute of Natural Science.

Farrar, Richard. 1973. *Birds of east-central Vermont.* Woodstock: Vermont Institute of Natural Science.

Laughlin, Sarah, and Douglas Kibbe. 1985. *The atlas of breeding birds of Vermont.* Hanover: University Press of New England.

Walton, Richard. 1988. *Bird finding in New England.* Boston: Godine.

Virginia

Wilds, Claudia, 1983. *Finding birds in the national capital area.* Washington, D.C.: Smithsonian Institution Press.

Washington

Dawson, W. L., and J. H. Bowles. 1909. *The birds of Washington.* Seattle: Occidental Publishing.

Hunn, Eugene. 1982. *Birding in Seattle and King County.* Seattle: Seattle Audubon Society.

Jewett, S. G., et al. 1953. *The birds of Washington State.* Seattle: University of Washington Press.

Larrison, Earl. 1952. *Field guide to the birds of Puget Sound.* Seattle: Seattle Audubon Society.

Larrison, Earl, and Klaus Sonnenberg. 1968. *Washington birds: Their location and identification.* Seattle: Seattle Audubon Society.

Lewis, Mark, and Fred Sharpe. 1987. *Birding the San Juan Islands.* Seattle: The Mountaineers.

Wahl, T. R., and D. R. Paulson. 1987. *A guide to bird finding in Washington.* Bellingham: Whatcom County Museum.

West Virginia

Hall, George. 1983. *West Virginia birds.* Pittsburgh: Carnegie Institute.

Wisconsin

Barger, N. R.; R. H. Lound; and S. D. Robbins. 1975. *Wisconsin birds.* Madison: University of Wisconsin Press.

Temple, Stanley, and John Cary. 1987. *Wisconsin birds.* Madison: University of Wisconsin.

Tessen, W. S. 1976. *Wisconsin's favorite bird haunts.* Madison: Wisconsin Society for Ornithology.

INDEX